William St. Chad Boscawen

**The Bible and the Monuments**

The Primitive Hebrew Records in the Light of Modern Research. Second Edition

William St. Chad Boscawen

**The Bible and the Monuments**

*The Primitive Hebrew Records in the Light of Modern Research. Second Edition*

ISBN/EAN: 9783744716574

Printed in Europe, USA, Canada, Australia, Japan

Cover: Foto ©Lupo / pixelio.de

More available books at **www.hansebooks.com**

FROM THE TEMPLE OF THE SUN-GOD AT SIPPARA, B.C. 900.
(*Photographed from the original.*)

THE

# BIBLE AND THE MONUMENTS.

### The Primitive Hebrew Records in the Light of Modern Research.

BY

W. ST. CHAD BOSCAWEN,

*Fellow of the Royal Historical Society, Member of the Society of Biblical Archæology.*

SECOND EDITION.

EYRE AND SPOTTISWOODE,

Her Majesty's Printers,

LONDON—GREAT NEW STREET, FLEET STREET, E.C.
EDINBURGH, GLASGOW, MELBOURNE, SYDNEY, & NEW YORK.

1895.

EYRE & SPOTTISWOODE,
*Her Majesty's Printers,*
DOWNS PARK ROAD, HACKNEY, N.E.

# PREFACE.

THE object of this work is best explained by its title; some statement, however, of its aims and plan may not be deemed unnecessary.

The East has ever been the land of surprises, and year after year the explorer and the decipherer are bringing to light treasures which for centuries have been buried beneath the dust of ages. The discoveries in Egypt, Assyria, and Babylonia have restored to us the inscribed records and monuments of great civilisations which preceded or existed concurrently with the Hebrew people and held contemporary intercourse with them. The history of the Hebrew people as recorded in the Old Testament has been found to be a part, and an important part, of the wider study of Oriental history. Events regarded formerly as merely incidents in the life of the Israelites are now seen to be but portions of greater and more widely extended popular movements, affecting the whole political area of the Oriental world. The migration of Abram, apparently a movement of a small tribal family from Ur of the

Chaldees, is now shown to be part of a vast heaving of the nations, extending from the banks of the Tigris to the lowlands of Egypt. The siege of Jerusalem by Sennacherib is no longer merely an event in Hebrew history, but an important item in the wider scheme of the establishment of Assyrian supremacy in Syria, during the long conflict between the rival powers of Egypt and Assyria. The recovery of the historical records of Egypt, Assyria, and Babylonia has given to the historical and prophetical books of the Old Testament an increased importance, and at the same time an increased responsibility, the test of historical accuracy.

It will be my aim in subsequent volumes of this series to show how the Hebrew record has vindicated its position in this respect. It is not only the question of *historical* accuracy that has to be established in the face of monumental evidence. The discovery and decipherment of the buried literature of Assyria and Babylonia have produced material which can be used also in the more difficult and delicate field of Biblical tradition, especially as to the *faithfulness* of these traditions, upon which the most fundamental doctrines of the Christian religion are based. The discovery of Babylonian versions of the Creation, the Fall, and the Deluge, and the story of the beginnings of civilisation, instituted a series of comparisons between monumental records, of admitted antiquity, and the Hebrew writings, a process the importance of which was beyond question.

The spirit of scepticism had not spared the traditions of the Old Testament, but sought to relegate them to the same land of myth and fable to which it had consigned the primitive traditions of Greece and Rome. Just at this crucial moment in the conflict, the grave mounds of Chaldea gave up their priceless stores of buried books with rich fragments of early traditions, marked with the indelible stamp of antiquity.

In this field of comparison with which this volume is concerned, a criticism of a very searching kind, impossible before, was rendered most applicable. The Babylonian legends of the primitive traditions, unlike the Indian, Egyptian, and others which had been used by sceptics, were written in a language, the sister if not the parent, of the Hebrew tongue. The test became then not one merely of mythological or poetic similarities, but extended into the closest philological comparison.

In this work I have placed before my readers the Babylonian and Assyrian versions of those traditions which are found in the early chapters of Genesis, and such comparisons are instituted as seemed to me to be within the range of fair criticism; and I have endeavoured to conduct this inquiry in as unbiassed a manner as possible. The Hebrew records, therefore, in this study are treated in exactly the same manner as the inscriptions from Babylonia, simply as the ancient literature of the Hebrew people. In what manner the comparison has tended to establish the authenticity and *faithfulness* of the Hebrew records, I leave my readers to form an opinion.

I have also purposely avoided any expression of opinion as to the date of the committal to writing of the Hebrew traditions. In this I have been guided by two reasons. In the first place this seemed to me to belong to a branch of Biblical criticism which I do not feel myself called upon, even were I to admit, which I do not, my competency, to express a definite opinion. No one is more convinced than I of the immense service rendered by the Higher Criticism to the right understanding of the construction of Hebrew literature, and without the critical analysis of the early chapters of Genesis, by Driver, Cheyne, Delitzsch, and others, the comparisons such as I have made would have been almost impossible. My second reason was based upon a conviction that the evidence at present accessible has not been established with sufficient clearness to enable us to express any dogmatic opinion. Fresh discoveries are ever being brought to light which necessitate often the complete revision of theories apparently perfectly tenable.

The discovery, for example, of the Tel el-Amarna Tablets is one which should make all scholars hesitate to regard any theory as permanent. Here an entirely new and powerful factor in Biblical criticism was suddenly brought to light, and demanded careful study from all. These tablets show that prior to the time of Moses, in the fifteenth century before Christ, there were studied in Egypt and in Canaan documents of a religious character from Babylonia. If scribes from Babylonia taught the cuneiform writing to the people of Canaan and to the learned in Jerusalem itself two centuries before Moses, may not the traditions which had been known to Abram five hundred years before in the land of Chaldea have been taught to priests in Canaanite cities? These tablets have shown us, as have the explorations of the Palestine Exploration Fund at Lacish (Tel Hesy), that there was a great and powerful civilisation and a literature among the Canaanites and the Amorites before the Israelites entered the land, and that they were not mere barbarians. To what extent this culture, almost entirely of Babylonian origin, affected the Hebrew people we do not know as yet; further research may have much in store for us. One fact however remains, which demands caution. There is now introduced into Biblical criticism a new, powerful, and hitherto unknown element, which may at any moment compel us to change entirely the theory which the present evidence seems to support. My object has been to place before my readers those monuments and inscriptions which seem to bear upon the early traditions of the Hebrew people, in order that they may have before them documentary evidence which has hitherto only been accessible to specialists.

# CONTENTS.

## CHAPTER I.

### THE HEBREW AND ASSYRIAN LANGUAGES.

Cuneiform writing—Phœnician culture—The home of the Semites—Early inscriptions—Sargon I., B.C. 3800—Legend of Sargon—Early trade and commerce—Hebrew and Assyrian languages—Primitive family names—Linguistic affinities—A curious piece of monumental evidence—Animal names—Royal names—Relationship of Assyrian to Hebrew—A royal prayer—India House inscription—Nebuchadnezzar's prayer—Hebrews in Chaldea . . . . . . . . . *Page* 17-36

## CHAPTER II.

### THE CREATION LEGENDS.

Discovery of the tablets—Assyrian libraries—Arrangement of the tablets—An Epic poem—Comparative table—Birth of the gods—The Divine Word—The Deep—The Hosts of Heaven—Babylonian Trinity—The Fifth Tablet—Celestial Orbs—A curious and striking parallel — Chaldean year — Babylonian Calendar and the Zodiac—Signs of the Zodiac—Seasons of the year—Festivals of the Sun-god—Babylonian Passover Feast—Moon worship—Religions of Nomad and Agriculturist—Dew and the rain—Hymns to the Moon-god of Ur—Hymns to the Sun-god—Reversal of the Hebrew order—The Gates of the Sun—Sinai and the Moon-god Sin—Feast of the New Moon—Divisions of the month—The Sabbath day—Is it lawful to heal on the Sabbath day?—The Sun to rule by day—Creation of Man—He shall have dominion—Creation of Woman—Origin of the tablets—Compilation—Tel el-Amarna Tablets—Older Creation

Legends—The Creation Legend of Eridu—Bel-Merodach as the Creator—Foundations of Assur—Gods and their sacred animals—A remarkable parallel—Legend of Kutha—Creation of evil—Chaldean Theologians . . . . . . 37-84

## CHAPTER III.

### THE SERPENT AND THE FALL.

War in Heaven—The enemy of the gods—The Serpent and magic—Temptation and the Fall—The Kerubim in Eden    85-90

## CHAPTER IV.

### THE BEGINNING OF CIVILISATION.

Cain and Abel—The land of Nod—Primitive Cities—Oannes the Fish-god—The harp and the organ—Metal working—The Fire Stick—Early bronze casting—Workers in iron in Palestine—Stories of the Shepherd and Gardener—Language and race—Foundation ceremonies — The position of women — Peaceful character—Sacred statues—General features . . . 91-108

## CHAPTER V.

### THE DELUGE.

The story's place in the Epic—Preservation of the Chaldean Noah—Names of the Sage—A bilingual tablet—COMPARATIVE TABLES (Chaldean and Hebrew)—Building of the Ark—Warning of the Deluge—Trying the Ark—Storing the Ark—Commencement of the Deluge—Entering the Ark—The great Deluge—Destruction of every living thing—Resting on the Mountain—Sending forth the dove—The swallow and the raven—The Sacrifice and the rainbow—Appeasing of Bel—No more Deluge—The everlasting Covenant—Tradition of Berosos—Comparison with Biblical narrative—Deluge a punishment for sin—The Trinity of destruction—The ship of Ea and the Ark—Provisioning the Ark—The Month of the Curse of Rain—Hymns of the Storm-gods — Resting-place of the Ark — The mountain not Ararat—Sending forth of the birds—The Bow of the Covenant—Translation of Samas-Napisti—Noah, Samas-Napisti, and Xisuthrus . . . . . . . . . 109-144

## CHAPTER VI.

### THE GRAVE AND THE FUTURE STATE.

*Page*

"The Book of the Dead"—Magicians and Sorcerers—Man and Nature—The Soul and Death—Ghosts and vampires—The chief ones of the earth—Mountain of the congregation—Sheol —The City of Death—Ruler of the Great City—The Bride of the Pit — The Land of No-Return — Naked and Bare — The Waters of Life — Weeping for Tammuz — Ah, my brother! Ah, sister!—Shadow of death—The worm enters—A place of punishment?—Immortality—Primitive ideas of Heaven—Pastoral Heaven—The Heaven of Anu—Guardians of Heaven—The food of life—The Robe of brightness—The Hebrew and Christian Heaven—Conclusion . . . . . . . 145-177

# REFERENCES TO SCRIPTURE TEXTS.

## GENESIS.

| Ch. Ver. | Page |
|---|---|
| 1. 1–5 | 41, 42 |
| 4 | 86 |
| 6–13 | 41 |
| 14–19 | 41, 48, 49 |
| 24, 25 | 70, 71 |
| 24–31 | 41 |
| 2. 1 | 46 |
| 2, 3 | 68 |
| 7 | 150 |
| 21, 22 | 72 |
| 3. 1 | 87 |
| 13 | 88 |
| 15 | 86 |
| 21 | 92 |
| 22 | 175 |
| 4. 3, 4 | 58 |
| 9 | 26 |
| 14 | 93 |
| 16 | 92 |
| 20 | 96 |
| 21 | 96 |
| 22 | 97, 99 |
| 5. 24 | 170 |
| 6. 14 | 134 |
| 15 | 134 |
| 14–16 | 131 |
| 18 | 131 |
| 6–9. – | 109, 114, 129 |
| 7. 3 | 131 |
| 4 | 131 |
| 7 | 131 |
| 16 | 131 |
| 8. 2 | 131 |
| 4 | 139 |
| 6–12 | 140 |
| 8–12 | 131 |
| 13 | 141 |
| 20 | 131 |
| 9. 13 | 134n., 142 |
| 13, 14 | 142 |
| 10. 10 | 94 |
| 11 | 18 |
| 11. 31 | 64 |
| 14. 1 | 93 |
| 21. 17 | 156n. |
| 23. – | 21 |
| 27. 28 | 59 |
| 28. 18 | 142n. |
| 42. – | 20 |

## EXODUS.

| Ch. Ver. | Page |
|---|---|
| 2. 5 | 134n. |
| 18. – | 26 |

## LEVITICUS.

| | |
|---|---|
| 16. – | 56 |
| 19. 26 | 88 |
| 23. 24, 25 | 57 |
| 25. 3–8 | 69 |

## NUMBERS.

| | |
|---|---|
| 1. 7 | 88 |
| 16. 30 | 167 |
| 22. 22 | 156n. |
| 28. 1 | 88 |

## DEUTERONOMY.

| | |
|---|---|
| 16. 9–16 | 69 |

## JUDGES.

| | |
|---|---|
| 14. 14 | 158 |

## 2 SAMUEL.

| | |
|---|---|
| 24. 15 | 133 |

## I KINGS.

| | |
|---|---|
| 7. 21 | 175 |
| 18. – | 137n. |

## 2 KINGS.

| | |
|---|---|
| 18. 30 | 157 |
| 21. 6 | 88 |
| 25. 27 | 56 |

## JOB.

| | |
|---|---|
| 3. 5 | 166 |
| 11. 8 | 167 |
| 12. 22 | 166 |
| 17. 14 | 167 |
| 21. 26 | 167 |
| 33. 18 | 166 |
| 38. 19 | 166 |
| 32 | 53 |
| 39. 9, 10 | 28 |

## PSALMS.

| | |
|---|---|
| 16. 11 | 176 |
| 18. 10 | 137n. |
| 22. 21 | 28 |

## Ch. Ver. Page

| | |
|---|---|
| 23. 1, 2 | 59 |
| 29. 6 | 28 |
| 45. 7 | 175 |
| 49. 16 | 166 |
| 55. 23 | 159 |

## PROVERBS.

| | |
|---|---|
| 8. 22–31 | 81 |

## ISAIAH.

| | |
|---|---|
| 13. 13 | 153 |
| 21 | 133 |
| 14. – | 31, 46 |
| 9 | 153, 154, 167 |
| 13 | 140 |
| 15 | 154 |
| 18. 4 | 59 |
| 34. 14 | 151 |
| 38. 17 | 159 |

## JEREMIAH.

| | |
|---|---|
| 14. 12 | 133 |
| 17. 1 | 142n. |
| 22. 18 | 164 |
| 27. 13 | 133 |

## EZEKIEL.

| | |
|---|---|
| 3. 9 | 142n. |
| 8. 14 | 163 |

## MICAH.

| | |
|---|---|
| 5. 6 | 109 |

## NAHUM.

| | |
|---|---|
| 3. 4 | 168 |

## ZECHARIAH.

| | |
|---|---|
| 12. 11 | 164 |

## MATTHEW.

| | |
|---|---|
| 12. 10 | 68 |
| 22. 11 | 175 |

## MARK.

| | |
|---|---|
| 1. 32 | 68 |

## REVELATION.

| | |
|---|---|
| 12. 7 | 85 |

# ILLUSTRATIONS.

## CHAPTER I.

|   | Page |
|---|---|
| MANEH WEIGHT . . . . . . . . | 20 |
| MACE HEAD OF SARGON I. (B.C. 3800), *full size* . . . | 22 |
| TABLET OF ASSUR-NAZIR-PAL I. (B.C. 1800) . . . . | 32 |
| INDIA HOUSE INSCRIPTION OF NEBUCHADNEZZAR II. (B.C. 606) . | 34 |

## CHAPTER II.

| FIRST CREATION TABLET, COPIED ABOUT B.C. 660 . . . | 42 |
|---|---|
| BOUNDARY STONE OF NEBUCHADNEZZAR I. (B.C. 1120) . . | 52 |
| TABLET FROM THE TEMPLE OF THE SUN-GOD AT SIPPARA (B.C. 900) . . . . . . . | *Frontispiece* |
| TABLETS FROM TEL EL-AMARNA (B.C. 1450) . . . . | 74 |
| EAGLE-HEADED FIGURE . . . . . | 82 |

## CHAPTER III

| MERODACH AND THE DRAGON . . . . . . | 86 |
|---|---|
| ASSYRIAN TABLET OF THE CREATION SERIES . . . . | 88 |
| SEAL OF THE TEMPTATION . . . . . . . | 90 |

## CHAPTER IV.

| | Page |
|---|---|
| *Ruins of the Palace of Gudea at Tello . . . . | 94 |
| *Harper and Choir (b.c. 3000) . . . . . . | 96 |
| Bronze Figures (b.c. 2800) and *Fire-god (b.c. 722) . . | 98 |
| *Statue of Gudea (b.c. 2800) . . . . . | 106 |

## CHAPTER V

| | |
|---|---|
| Deluge Tablet (Portion of the Eleventh Tablet) . . | 110 |
| ,, ,, No. 2 . . . . . . | 116 |
| Jackal-headed god . . . . . | 134 |
| Seal representing Chaldean Noah . . . . . | 142 |

## CHAPTER VI.

| | |
|---|---|
| Winged Human-Headed Lion . . . . . | 158 |

[*All the Illustrations, with the exception of those marked \*, have been reproduced from photographs taken by Messrs. Eyre and Spottiswoode from the originals.*]

# THE
# BIBLE AND THE MONUMENTS.

## CHAPTER I.

### THE HEBREW AND ASSYRIAN LANGUAGES.

THE comparisons which we may institute in this work, and the illustrations which we shall derive from the monuments of Assyria and Babylonia, will be of far more importance if we bear in mind the fact of the close relationship which exists between the language of the monuments and that of the Holy Scriptures.

The languages of the Assyrian inscriptions and of the records from Babylonia are branches of the great group of the Semitic tongues, and therefore older sisters of the Hebrew and Arabic. Coming to us, as they do, with a far greater antiquity and with a more varied vocabulary, derived from vast stores of secular as well as sacred literature, they cannot help but be valuable store-houses for the student of the Hebrew writings, when he has recognised the close affinity which exists both in vocabulary and in grammatical construction.

The ancient Semitic dialects of the Tigro-Euphrates valley were two in number; the northern, that of the people of Assyria, a colony from the southern mother-land of Babylonia (Gen. 10. 11); the other, that of the Semitic population of Babylonia. There are slight dialect variations between them, but they do not amount to as much as exists between the dialects of a northern and western English county. The Assyrian may be said to be the more Semitic of the two, being brought less in contact with foreign elements, and especially with the ancient Akkadians, or Turanian inhabitants of Southern Babylonia, who had exercised great influence on the older tongue of the Babylonian Semites. The Semitic dialect of Babylonia, although probably not the parent tongue of this linguistic family, is represented by numerous inscribed records of every class, which carry us back to the remote antiquity of thirty-nine centuries before the Christian era (B.C. 3800); and even these records afford evidence of a far more remote antiquity. The whole system of the cumbrous cuneiform writing, its elaborate syllabary, the use of polyphones, and the numerous ideograms, all tend to show clearly that this writing was not the invention of the Semites. The method of the Semitic mind, as exhibited in the invention of the Phœnician alphabet from the more complex hieratic script of Egypt, and in their treatment of the cuneiform writing, is always clearly shown to be towards simplification; and to credit them with the invention of the cuneiform writing, with its hundreds of ideograms and compound signs, is a direct contradiction of this faculty.

There is, however, another powerful element in the Semitic character which has been, and still is, a most important factor in their national life; it is that of adaptability. Inventors they have never shown themselves to be: but wherever we find them, from their first appearance in

Chaldea some five or six thousand years ago even until the present day, we find them exhibiting this wonderful characteristic of adaptability to the manners, customs, and language of those about them. In religion, in art,—indeed there is, strictly speaking, no Semitic art,—in all the essential features of settled civilisation, as distinguished from the simple wants of nomad life, we find them indebted to those with whom they came in contact. In Babylonia they adopted the polytheistic pantheon of the Akkadians along with their own simple monotheism; but simplified it, arranging its confused elements, and producing the small but comprehensive pantheon of Assyria. In Phœnicia is found the same borrowing in art as in religion; from the teachings of the Egyptian, the Babylonian, the Hittite, and, later still, the Greek, all contributing to form that powerful but *bizarre* school of Phœnician art, which exercised so great an influence on the world's artistic development. As in art, so in religion: the theogony of Phœnicia is a product of all the religious schools of Western Asia, Egypt, and the Isles of the Sea combined.

It has been necessary to digress thus far from the purely linguistic portion of the subject in order to understand the reasons which led the Semites of Babylonia to adopt this cumbrous writing, so different in form and mechanism from that of the Hebrews, Phœnicians, and Arameans.

The home of the Semites must be placed in the desert pastures of Central Arabia, whence they had been attracted to the fertile plains of Shinar, or Sumir, the garden of South Babylonia, where a highly-developed civilisation already existed. The great walled cities, with temples, palaces, and lofty seven-staged observatory towers, were indeed strange to them; so strange, that we find they had no word for city, the word used in the inscriptions being *alu*, a word cognate with the Hebrew *ohel*, "a tent." To the true nomad the tent was his house and his city, the largest elaboration of this being the *ohel m'oed*, "the tent of assembly," the Tabernacle of the Wanderings. Two causes mainly contributed to their entry into Babylonia—famine and trade. Centuries before Israel cried "There is corn in Egypt!" (Gen. 42) these weary wanderers had turned their steps towards the richly-watered plains of Babylonia. The second element which induced this settlement in the land was that of trade, and this was indeed the more powerful. The earliest Semitic words to be found in the inscriptions are those relating to trade, *simu*, "price," the Arabic *sam*, represented by an ideogram borrowed from the Akkadian, composed of "corn and measure," indicating the former use of a corn tariff. In the same manner the *mana* "weight" (the Hebrew *maneh*) was introduced into the commercial and religious texts by them as early as B.C. 4000. A still more interesting change, however, is to be noticed in the employment of a new word for town, namely, *makhazu*, which is the Talmudic *makhaza*, "a market town." In addition to these two striking indications, it is important to notice that the earliest bilingual lesson books used for instruction in the schools of Babylonia, and subsequently in the schools of Assyria, were those which contained simple commercial phrases; the Akkadian in one column, the Semitic in the other. It may be interesting to give here an extract from one of these early examples of an Ollendorf. This tablet is one of a class known as *Ana itti šu*, "to be with him," literally, "Hand-books."

MANEH WEIGHT.
(*Photographed from the original.*)

In the following extract is given the Semitic version only, but it should be borne in mind that this is side by side with the Akkadian:—

*Makiru*, "the tariff."
*Makiru rabu*, "the great tariff."
*Makiru zikhru*, "the small tariff."
*Makiru enšu*, "the short tariff."
*Makiru malu*, "the full tariff."
*Makiru dannu*, "the strong tariff."
*Makiru kinu*, "the fixed tariff."
*Makiru tabu*, "the good tariff."
*Makiru bašu*, "the existing tariff."

The slightest acquaintance with Hebrew will enable the student to recognise here the close relationship with the language of the Scriptures. *Makiru* is the Hebrew *mekir*, and the other words are all to be found in an ordinary Hebrew lexicon. An extract from a deed of this same class may be quoted on account of the important light which it throws on some of the earliest records of Hebrew life: *Aššu ẓibat kaspi šu bit ekil gan ardu amat ana man-zazani usziz*—"Concerning the loan of his silver (money), a house, field, garden, man-servant and maid-servant for security he places." Here is all the wealth of a typical Hebrew home, "the house, the land, the male and female servants." With such carefully-drawn deeds as this in use before he left his Chaldean home, is it any wonder that the transaction of the purchase of the cave of Machpelah is carried out with such commercial accuracy (Gen. 23).

The Semites had borrowed the writing and the chief elements of civilisation from their Akkadian neighbours as early as B.C. 3800, as is proved by an important inscription on a mace head of Sargon I., now in the British Museum. The inscription upon this small but priceless record reads : *Šargani šar alu Agadhe ana* (*Ilu*) *Šamaš in Sippara Amuru*—"Sargon, king of the city of Akkad; to the Sun-god (Samas) in the city of Sippara, I approached (looked)."

The age of Sargon is certainly one of the most remarkable periods in the history of Babylonia. Its very importance is shown by the fact that there has grown up a series of legends connected with the hero and his times, which show how highly he was regarded by the writers of later times. Sargon of Akkad was to Babylonia the great ethnic hero of the Semites, and many of the legends connected with him present remarkable parallels to those of both Hebrew and classical writers. One of the most remarkable of these is the story of his birth, which in its surroundings presents many features closely resembling the story of Moses. The story of the birth and childhood of Sargon is preserved in a tablet in the British Museum. Here we are told, "My little mother (*umminitum*) my father did not know, my father's brother ruled in the mountains. In the city of Atsu pirani which is on the banks of the Euphrates, she conceived and brought me forth—my little mother bore me in a secret place, she placed me in a basket of reeds, with bitumen she closed its mouth. She gave me to the river, which did not cover over me, but carried me to Akki the irrigator." The tablet then describes how this irrigator brought the hero up as a gardener, and that the goddess Istar prospered him in his work, and eventually he became king of the land. He then conquers the land, uniting all the country under one rule, with the new capital of Akkad as its centre. In other documents of this king we have his conquests described, and although there is a certain amount of as-

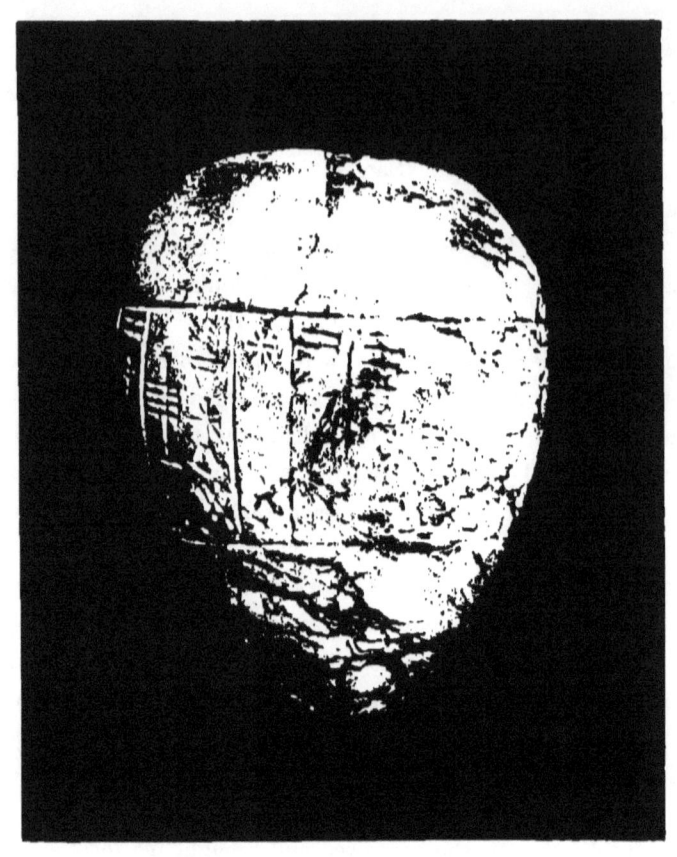

Mace Head of Sargon I., b.c. 3800 (*full size*).
(*Photographed from the original.*)

trological and astronomical matter, there is certainly a historical basis to the account. The most important of these campaigns is the expedition of Sargon to the land of Amurri, and to the land in the midst of the Sea of the Rising-Sun, where he remained three years, and set up his statue. Now this can have no other meaning than the conquest of Syria and the advance of the Babylonian armies to Cyprus. Confirmation of this is given by the discovery of seals of Naram-Sin, the son of Sargon, in Cyprus, and more strongly by the action of Sargon II. (B.C. 722), who, on his conquest of Cyprus, made a special object of setting up his statue near to Larnaka, with an inscription recording his conquests upon it. This statue is now in the Royal Museum at Berlin. A special interest is attached to this expedition, as it was the first contact between the West and Chaldea, and was not without influence which remained until later ages.

The second expedition of this period was even of greater importance, namely, that to the land of Magan, the Sinaitic Peninsula. From the earliest times there seems to have been an intercourse by sea between Chaldea and the Sinaitic Peninsula, chiefly maintained for the purpose of obtaining hard stones, such as diorite and porphyry for the making of the statues of the kings, and for timber of a more durable kind than the palm-wood of Babylonia. This trade brought both Southern Arabia and Egypt by the Coptos route in contact with Chaldea, and the commercial activity of the period seems to have been very great. Two other products of the Sinaitic Peninsula especially attracted the attention of the Babylonian rulers,—these were copper and the turquoise. Towards the latter end of the reign of Sargon, the Chaldean rulers determined to obtain possession of the rich mineral regions of the Peninsula of Sinai, and an expedition was organised under Sargon, and continued by his son Naram-Sin, which resulted in the conquest of the region and the acquisition of the mines. This was a most important event, for the Chaldeans seem to have held the mines for at least half a century, when they were expelled by Senefru, the builder of the Pyramid of Medum, and founder of the fourth Egyptian dynasty, about B.C. 3700.

In addition to the extensive military-commercial power of Chaldea at this period, it seems also to have been an age when the affairs of the nation were organised. It is to this period that the first compilation of astronomical works was assigned, and Sargon certainly had a library with scribes in his royal city of Agadhe. So that it was a period in Chaldean history which presents some considerable resemblance to the position of Moses in Hebrew literature.

We can fix the date of this ancient ruler with remarkable accuracy by means of inscriptions preserved in the British Museum. In the cylinder of Nabonidus, a king who was noted for his great antiquarian zeal in his search for ancient records, we read as follows:— "I sought for its old foundation stone, and eighteen cubits deep (30 feet) I dug into the ground, and the foundation stone of Naram-Sin the son of Sargon, which for 3,200 years no king who had preceded me had seen, the Sun-god, the great lord of the House of Light, the temple of the abode of the pleasure of his heart, let me see, even me." Had this far-reaching date appeared in the inscription of any other king than Nabonidus, who was so accurate in all his other statements, it might have been doubted, but this can hardly be so now. The restoration of this temple took place in or about the king's sixth year, B.C. 550-49, which would make the date of Naram-Sin, B.C. 3750; and as Sargon is credited with a reign of 45 years, his date, therefore, is about 3,800 years before our era. That the Semites had already borrowed the cuneiform writing, and established a literary class, may be concluded from the fact that in the collection of M. de Clercq, in Paris, is the seal of *Ibni-Šarru* (the king has made), "the tablet writer" of Sargon.

Having once acquired the art of writing this active-minded race made rapid progress, and by the time of Khammurabi (B.C. 2235), a monarch contemporary with Abram, they had an extensive literature, partly original and partly consisting of translations or adaptations of the older Akkadian folk lore.

Having established the early date and nature of the contact between the once nomad Semite, and the settled, plodding and inventive Akkadian, it may be well to consider a comparison between the language of the Old Testament and that of the Semitic inscriptions of Assyria and Babylonia. The comparisons made will do more than show a philological relationship between Assyrian and Hebrew; they will, aided by the rich stores of lexicographical matter in the long-buried libraries, enable the student to explain words of which it was hitherto difficult to ascertain the derivation.

## Domestic Life.

In family life there is the word *abu*, "father," a word common to all branches of the Semitic family, as is also *ummu*, "mother." *Ablu*, "son," preserved in the Hebrew *Abel*, and derived from the verb *abalu*, "to flow"—the son proceeding from the father. *Bintu* and *binatu*, "daughter," are both cognate with Arabic *bint* and the Hebrew *banoth*, "daughters." *Akhu*, "brother," the Hebrew *akh*, and explained in the tablets by the synonyms of "side," and "to protect"—the brother being the one who stood by the side of another, and whose duty it was to guard him, which throws singular light upon the passage. "Am I my brother's keeper?" (Gen. 4. 9.) Cognate to another word, also of great importance, namely, *khatanu*, "father-in-law," is the Hebrew *khatan*, as in Exod. 18, &c. This word is derived from *khatanu*, "to protect," because, according to the old Semitic law of matriarchy, the man married into his wife's family, as did Moses and Jacob, and the wife's father became his protector. So also the word *sibu*, "the grandfather" (Heb. *sebah*), which means "the grey-haired one"; the town council, the βουλη of the Greeks, called *sibuti*, "the grey-haired ones." Lastly, the word for the family itself, *kimtu*—derived from *kamu*, "to bind"—the family being the small circle of individuals united by the tie of relationship. This word is preserved in the word *kimmah* of Job, the family of the Pleiades.

The close relationship between the tongues may also be seen by the comparison of the following series of the commoner words of every-day life:—

| Assyrian. | Hebrew. | Meaning. |
| --- | --- | --- |
| *Resu* | *Res* | Head |
| *Kakkadu* | *Kodkod* | Head |
| *Inu* | *Ain* | Eye |
| *Appu* | *Af* | Face or Nose |
| *Pu* | *Pi* | Mouth |
| *Saptu* | *Safa* | Lip |
| *Usnu* | *Ozen* | Ear |
| *Panu* | *Paneh* | Face |

| Assyrian—cont. | Hebrew—cont. | Meaning—cont. |
|---|---|---|
| Lisanu | Lason | Tongue |
| Idu | Yad | Hand |
| Katu | — | Hand |
| Birka | Birkaim | Knees |
| Zumbi | Zanab | Tail |
| Libbu | Leb | Heart |
| Pagaru | Peger | Corpse |

In the same degree will be noticed a near relationship between the words relating to the elements of nature:—

| Assyrian. | Hebrew. | Meaning. |
|---|---|---|
| Šamu } Šâmamu | Samaim | Heaven |
| Irtsitu | Erez | Earth |
| Naru | Nahr | River |
| Agammu | Agam | Marsh |
| Tiamtu | Tehom | Sea |
| Me | Maim | Water |
| Šamaš | Šemes | Sun |
| Kakabu | Kokab | Star |
| Yumu | Yom | Day |
| Uru | Or | Light |
| Nuru | Ner | Light |
| Lilatu | Lailah | Night |
| Birku | Barak | Lightning |
| Abnu | Eben | Stone |

From the above short vocabularies it is apparent how close is the agreement between the language of the inscriptions and that of the Old Testament.

ANIMAL LIFE.

The words selected from the inscriptions, dating from so remote an antiquity, have a value beyond that of philological study. This is especially the case in regard to words relating to animal life, as from these the student is able to picture the home and surroundings of the people, and to note the introduction of foreign words, which is the result of contact with other nations. In the zoological vocabulary of the Semites of Babylonia many words common to the whole group of the Semitic family may be found; but here and there words occur which, by their variation, become of importance.

Among the animals known to the Semites before their disruption, we find the domestic "ox," *alpu*, the Hebrew *elif*, as distinct from *remu*, the "wild ox," the mistranslated unicorn (*reem*) of the Authorised Version (Job 39. 9, 10; Pss. 22. 21 & 29. 6, &c.). This animal is the wild ox so frequently represented on the monuments of the middle Assyrian Empire. With regard to the existence of the wild ox, the *Bos primogenus*, in Western Asia, there is a curious piece of monumental evidence which seems to have escaped the notice of scholars. The bull hunts in Assyria are frequently represented in the sculptures of the early Assyrian kings, and in those of Assur-nazir-pal (B.C. 885), but we find no trace of them after that date. Had the animal become extinct in the days of Sargon II. (B.C. 722) and his successors? The word *zinu*, "sheep," the Hebrew *zon*, is generally used in a collective plural form *zeni*, "sheep," equivalent to "the flock." The goat, especially the he-goat, was called *atudu*, Hebrew *attud*. In the old Akkadian, which exhibits a wonderful power of word-building in its nomenclature, the goat is called by the name *si-ak-ka*, the "horn-raising" animal. The camel was also known, and called by the name of *gamalu*, the Hebrew *gamal*; which is interesting if taken with the root *gamalu*, "to benefit," the camel being "the benefactor" of the true nomad tribe. The ass also was known by the name of *imiru*, in Hebrew *khamor*. The "horse" by the name of *susu*, Hebrew *sus*; but it is difficult to say if the word may not be of foreign origin, as it is explained in the inscriptions by the name of the "animal of the east," or the "mountains." This would seem to connect it with the districts to the east of the Tigris, the regions of the Elamite kingdom, with its capital of Susan, and later still the seat of the Persian rule, whence we get the second Hebrew name of *Parash*, connected with Fars, or Persia. The last animal to be noticed as of the domesticated class is the dog, *kalbu*, the Hebrew *keleb*, which would seem among the Semites, as among the Aryans, to have been one of the first companions of man.

The list of wild animals known to the Babylonian Semites is an interesting one, and throws great light on Biblical zoology.

In this portion of the subject I am much indebted to the studies of the Rev. W. Houghton on the "Mammalia of the Assyrian Sculptures" (*Trans. Bibl. Arch. Soc.*, vol. v.), and from his work is taken the following list of names:—

| Assyrian. | Hebrew. | Meaning. |
| --- | --- | --- |
| *Udumu* | *Adam* | Ape |
| *Dassu* | *Dishôn* | Antelope |
| *Dabu* | *Dôb* | Bear |
| *Guzalu* | *Ázal* (Arab.) | Gazelle |
| *Zabi* | *Zĕbî* | Gazelle |
| *Zaparu* | *Zaphir* | Wild Goat |
| *Annabu* | *Arnebeth* | Hare |
| *Akhu* | *Oakh* | Jackal or Hyena |
| *Nimru* | *Nâmêr* | Leopard |
| *Nesu* | *N'aas* (Arab.) | Lion |
| *Parie* | *Pere* | Wild Ass |
| *Zibu* | *Zeêb* | Wolf |

Sufficient evidence has been given of the remarkable agreement in vocabulary between the Assyrian and Hebrew to show that Assyrian may be regarded as the elder sister of the Hebrew tongue.

In grammar, as in vocabulary, Assyrian presents a most striking agreement with Hebrew and the cognate Semitic dialects. Assyrian may be said to be nearest in relation to Hebrew and Phœnician, the two leading north Semitic tongues, with some close affinities with the Ethiopic. It differs most from the Aramaic and the later dialects, but, strangely enough, exhibits some most striking affinities in its grammar to the Arabic. The Assyrian grammar presents all the fulness of the Arabic in the employment of secondary and tertiary verbal conjugations, and the consequent elaborate power of word-building, as well as the preservation of the *mimation*—similar to Arabic *nunnation* in both verbal and nominal endings—all attest this similarity. The employment of the same ground forms of verbal conjugations as in Hebrew, the similarity of construction and expression, all render Assyrian easy of acquirement by those who have mastered the elements of Hebrew study, and therefore entitle it to recognition at the hands of Biblical students and teachers.

SEMITIC LITERATURE.

In addition to the value of Assyrian as a cognate language with that of the Bible, it presents a still more important critical aid, in the form of its valuable lexicography. The scribes of the Babylonian temples and the Royal Library at Nineveh resemble, in many respects, the Sanscrit grammarians of India. They studied their language and its literature from the points of philologists and critics. They compiled dictionaries and commentaries, and it is from these that so much valuable information is gained. One example of this class furnishes most interesting synonyms and explanations.

The word *sarru*, king—the Hebrew *sar*, prince—is derived from the verb *sararu*, " to be bright, brilliant, shining," and so in a list of synonyms may be obtained the following equivalents for this word :—

*Malku*  } = Hebrew *melek*, prince.
*Maliku* }

*Lulimu* = A borrowed word, the equivalent of the word *ailu*, " the bell wether " or " leader," the *alim* of Isa. 14.

*Parakku* = " The veiled one," the equivalent of the Hebrew *paroketh*, the " veil of the Temple " ; the king being the centre of the harem or exclusive portion of the palace.

*Ebilu* = " The ruler," a form of Hebrew *baal*.

*Ri'hu* = " Prince," the Hebrew *reu'*.

*Enu* = " Lord," borrowed from the Akkadian *en*, " Lord."

In the same list there are several other interesting words, such as *Milkatum* = *Sarratum*, the equivalence between the Hebrew *Milcah* and *Sarah*. The study of such valuable lists as these, of which the above quoted is only one among many, will enable the student to clear up many obscure passages in the Bible, and to ascertain with greater accuracy the true meanings of words of rare occurrence.

The advantages of the comparison between the Assyrian monuments and inscriptions are not, however, confined solely to the ground of philology. The two literatures, both the product of the Semitic mind, have much in common, and, as we shall see, the same lofty ideas of the Divinity, the same conception of sin; and thus the Biblical student will find on the shelves of the Assyrian libraries much that will aid him in his studies, especially in the field of comparative religion.

As an example of the value of these Assyrian texts for comparison with Hebrew literature, may be cited the following beautiful prayer of Assur-nazir-pal I., the son of Samsi-Rimman, whose reign may be placed about B.C. 1800, five centuries before the time of Moses. The text and translation of this hymn has been published by Mr. R. E. Brünnow, in the *Zeitschrift für Assyriologie* (vol. v., 69):—

> To the lady of Nineveh, the exalted one of the gods,
> The daughter of the Moon, the sister of the Sun,
> Who reigns over all realms!
> To her who determines decrees, the goddess of the whole earth;
> To the lady of Heaven and Earth, who receives prayers;
> To her who hearkens unto pleading and takes hold of petitions!
> To the merciful goddess who loves justice! *
> Istar, everything that is disturbed distresses her!
> Oh, for the afflictions which I behold, I weep before thee!
> To my words full of sighing direct thy ears!
> To my afflicted cry let thy mind be open!
> Look upon me, Oh lady, that through thy turning towards me
>    the heart of thy servant may become strong.†
> I am Assur-nazir-pal, thy afflicted servant,
> Humble, adoring thy divinity, watchful, thy favourite!
> Who approved the freewill offering, who without intermission
>    offers thy sacrifices;
> Who delights in thy festivals, who restores thy shrines;

---

\* Cp. Ps. 4. 1; 27. 7; 28. 2.   † Cp. Ps. 80. 3, 7, 9.

Tablet of Assur-nazir-pal I., b.c. 1800.
(*Photographed from the original.*)

# A ROYAL PRAYER.

Who makes plentiful the wine, the joy of thy heart, which
thou lovest ! *
The son of Samsi-Rimman who adored the great gods.
I was begotten in the midst of the mountains of which none
knoweth ;
I was unlearned, and to thy ladyship never did I pray !
The people of Assyria also, and did not draw near to thy
divinity !
But thou, Oh Istar, mighty princess of the gods,
In the lifting up of thine eyes didst thou teach me,† and didst
desire my rule !
Thou didst take me from the mountains and didst call me to the
threshold of men !
Thou didst preserve for me the sceptre of righteousness ‡ until
the growing old of all mankind.
And thou, Oh Istar, didst make great my name !
Thou hast granted unto the faithful salvation and mercy.§
Out of thy mouth went forth the decree, to make anew the gods.
The temples which were falling in I repaired,
The fallen gods I built up, and restored to their places ;

(*Some lines too mutilated.*)

In what have I sinned against thee ?
Why hast thou allotted me diseases, boils, and pestilence ?
Is this thy just decree ?
As one who did honour to thy divinity (am I afflicted).
If I have not committed sin and evil why am I thus (smitten) ?
In my foundations I am unloosened . . . . .
I am broken in pieces,‖ and rest I find not
On the throne of my kingdom. I fasted, and
To the feast I had prepared I drew not near !
The wine of the libation turned to gall.

---

* Cp. " Wine which cheereth God and man " (Judg. 9. 13).
† Cp. Ps. 4. 6, " In the lifting up of thy countenance."
‡ Cp. " The sceptre of thy kingdom is a right sceptre " (Ps. 45. 6).
§ Cp. Ps. 3. 8, " Salvation belongeth unto the Lord "; also Ps. 119. 155.
‖ Cp. Isa. 30. 14 ; Ps. 2. 9.

From rejoicing I am withheld, and from the beauties and
pleasures of life I am cut off.
My eyes are sealed up, I cannot see:
I do not lift them up from the surface of the earth!
How long, Oh lady! shall the disease without ceasing destroy
my members?
I, Assur-bani-pal, thy adorer,
Who lays hold of the sceptre of thy divinity, who prays to
thy ladyship,
Look upon me with compassion, and let me pray to thy nobility!
In whatsoever thou art angry, grant me forgiveness, and let
thy mind be purged:
Let mercy in thy heart be strong upon me!
Let affliction come forth, and sin be restrained;
Oh, lady! from thy mouth let my tranquillity come forth.
The Priest-King, thy beloved, who never changes,
Grant him mercy, and remove his affliction!
Oh, pray for him to thy beloved, the father of the gods!

By a comparison of the above poem with the references given in the footnotes, it will be observed there are many phrases of striking similarity to the Hebrew Psalms.

One other extract of a much later date may be added for the sake of comparison. The prayer of Nebuchadnezzar II. (B.C. 606), written during the time that Israel was in captivity, affords a striking example of the religious literature of the period, and is wonderfully rich in its pure Semitic thought and religious aspirations. The following extract, taken from the long inscription of Nebuchadnezzar now in the India House Museum, forms the concluding lines of the last column, and is the king's prayer to Merodach:—

To Merodach my lord I prayed and lifted up my hand. Oh Merodach, firstborn of the gods, mighty prince, who didst create me, and hast entrusted to me the sovereignty over hosts of men; as my own

INDIA HOUSE INSCRIPTION OF NEBUCHADNEZZAR II., B.C. 606.
(*Photographed from the original.*)

precious life I do love the nobility of the divinity. In all the habitable earth I have seen no city fairer than thy city of Babylon. As I have loved the reverence of thy great divinity, and have sought (ever) after thy divinity, accept the lifting up of my hands, for I the king am thy adorer, who pleases thy heart. Appointed a priest-king (to be) the restorer of all thy cities. By thy command, oh Merodach, merciful one, may this temple which I have made endure for ever.

A second prayer, which is even more beautiful, is found on a clay cylinder :—

To Merodach my lord I prayed, I began to him my petition. The words of my heart sought for him; and I said, Oh prince, that art from everlasting, lord of all that exists, for the king whom thou lovest, whom thou callest by name, as it seemeth good unto thee thou guidest his name aright, thou watchest over him in the path of righteousness! I, the prince who obeys thee, am the work of thy hands; thou hast created me, and hast entrusted to me the sovereignty over hosts of men; according to thy goodness, O lord, thou hast made me to pass over them all. Let me love thy supreme lordship, let the fear of thy divinity exist in my heart, and give what seemeth good unto thee, for thou upholdest my life. Then he, the firstborn of the gods, Merodach the prince, heard my prayer and accepted my petition.

These extracts may prove sufficient to show how high was the religious development of Babylonia during the period when the *élite* of the Hebrew nation were mingling with the wise men of Chaldea; and it is from these valuable contemporary documents that we are able to estimate the forces which tended, in no slight degree, to bring about the most marvellous national *renaissance* which the world has ever known.

In conclusion, it should be remembered that the two most important periods in the life of the Hebrew nation are both associated with Chaldea. From Ur of the Chaldees the national ancestor came to the Land of Promise after a long contact with the earlier civilisation; and it was during the golden age of the empire, in the days of Nebuchadnezzar and his successors, there was kindled that wonderful national patriotism in the Hebrew heart which centuries of banishment and persecution failed to crush. It is therefore, most important that at the commencement of this study the affinities of the language and thought of the nations of the Tigro-Euphrates valley and Judea should be borne in mind.

It is this close relationship between the Hebrew people and the inhabitants of Assyria and Chaldea which renders the comparisons between the ancient literatures of these empires and the Scriptures of such great value. We have shewn in this chapter that, racially and linguistically, the Hebrews and the ancient Semitic people of the Tigro-Euphrates valley were closely allied. Their language reveals the fact that at one time they had occupied a common home, and that, the cradle-land of the Semitic race. It is therefore not difficult to suppose that during this long period of intercourse traditions of the beginnings of all things were formulated, and were the common property of the Hebrews and Babylonians. How many points in common there were between these traditions and the Hebrew version we shall see in the subsequent chapters.

## CHAPTER II.

### THE CREATION LEGENDS.

UNTIL the discovery and decipherment of the Assyrian inscriptions, there was very little material with which to compare the Hebrew account of the Creation of the World. Its simplicity was so marked, that it was far removed from the confused polytheistic traditions of Babylonia and Phœnicia, as recorded by the Greco-Chaldean priest Berosos and the Phœnician priest Sanchoniathon. The former of these authors certainly resided at Babylon in the third century before our era, at a period when the temple of Belus was still in existence, and when no doubt some portion of the library remained, but the traditions which he has recorded are evidently derived from more than one source, and are therefore much confused. With regard to the Phœnician traditions, they are of still less use for comparative purposes, being certainly of late origin, and, like all products of the Phœnician mind, exhibiting the influence of foreign religious teaching. We know of this cosmogony only through the works of Philo of Byblus, a writer in the early Christian era, and whose literary work is of small value. His style is complicated and confused, his matter of little worth; he mixes together in the most absurd manner the mythologies of Egypt, Babylonia, and Greece, in his pretended Phœnician cosmogony. His etymological explanations of the various names shows that he had no knowledge of the languages from which they were derived.

STORY OF THEIR DISCOVERY.

In the year 1874, a most important and startling discovery was made by the patient labours of Mr. George Smith. He had already two years previously given to students that important document the "Chaldean Account of the Deluge," which may be called the Magna Charta of Assyriology, and which at once showed Biblical students the valuable aid they might expect from the clay tablets of the buried libraries of Nineveh and Babylon. He supplemented his first discovery by the publication of the Babylonian Legends of the Creation, which were at once seen to present a close resemblance to the Mosaic account. The first translations published by him were naturally merely tentative, but during the period that has elapsed since their first publication Assyriology has made great progress, and our knowledge of the Assyrian language and literature has become wider and more accurate.

This important series of documents, alas, still too fragmentary, have been studied by almost all the leading Assyriologists, in England by Professor Sayce, Mr. Pinches and myself, on the Continent by such able scholars as Drs. Oppert, Schrader, and Delitzsch; the result has been, that hidden meanings and niceties of expression have been brought out, and an almost general concensus of agreement established.

The tablets come from the royal library of Assurbanipal at Nineveh; they are copies written about the year B.C. 660, by order of the king, and placed in the temple library which he established there "for the instruction of his people." This temple-library was manifestly a copy in every respect of the great library in the temple of Nebo—the god of learning—in Borsippa, and most of its documents were copies of older works deposited there. It was called by the same name and dedicated to the same god, as is shown by the following endorsement upon one of the tablet books, which reads, "According to the copies of the tablets of Assyria and Akkad, on tablets I have written and explained, and in the inner chamber of E-Zida, the temple of Nebo, my Lord, which is in Nineveh, I have placed; for the pleasure of Nebo. The King of the hosts of Heaven and Earth look with joy upon this chamber, and support by day the head of Assurbanipal, the worshipper of thy divinity; and grant this prayer."

The statement that these tablets were copies of older documents in the libraries of Babylonia, naturally made scholars anxious for the time when the spade of the explorer should rescue from the ruins of the older empire earlier editions of these important texts.

The desire has been fortunately met, and we have now both duplicates and additional fragments from the libraries of both Borsippa and Sippara (Sepharvaim), as well as portions of a still older legend from the ancient priest-city of Kutha. These Babylonian copies are of great importance, as they cannot have been taken from the Assyrian tablets, which were probably buried at the time of the fall of Nineveh, but are from older copies in their own libraries. They are most valuable also because of certain variants they afford, which explain obscure passages.

There appear to have been seven tablets in the series—corresponding to the number of the days of Genesis—but the Babylonian arrangement seems to be rather that of a series of acts of creation, and the days and tablets do not correspond exactly.

The arrangement of the tablets is according to the usual system of Assyrian and Babylonian libraries, namely, that of classifying them by number and by the first words of the first tablet of the series. We find a curious resemblance to this in the Hebrew system by which the books of the Pentateuch are arranged. The first words of the First Tablet are *Enu-va Elis*, "When on High," or "In the time when on High," and so we find the Fourth and Fifth Tablets endorsed, "Tablet IV. or V., *Enu-va Elis*." This system agrees exactly with that of the Hebrew scribes, who called the first three books of Moses by their opening words: Genesis, בְּרֵאשִׁית " *Bereshith*," " In the Beginning "; Exodus, שְׁמוֹת "*Shemoth* "; and Leviticus, וַיִּקְרָא " *Wayyikra*." Indeed, as the Canon was not drawn up until after the Babylonian Captivity, we may with reason suppose this convenient system of classification to have been borrowed from the Babylonian scribes.

We now possess portions of the First, Second, Third, Fourth, Fifth, and Seventh Tablets of the series, and can form a very fair idea of the character of the work of which we may conclude the separate tablets formed chapters.

As is natural with a work emanating from a polytheistic and philosophical religious school, such as that of the Babylonian priesthood, the Chaldean account is much longer and more poetic in character than the Hebrew record. Indeed, the suggestion of Professor Sayce that it was treated in the form of a species of epic poem, similar to the Legends of Gilgames,[*] seems a very tenable one.

---

[*] This name, formerly read as Gizdhubar, is now read Gilgames, but there is little doubt tha this Chaldean hero was the Nimrod of the Jewish and Arab legends.

It is impossible to group the tablets in parallel correspondence to the Hebrew days of Creation, but they may be roughly arranged in the following order :—

Tablet I.—The Pre-creative State and the First Day (Gen. 1. 1–5).

Tablets II., III., IV.—The Creation of Light and the war between light and darkness. The victory of the former and the separation of Heaven and Earth, the banishment of the Dragon of Chaos to the depths of the under world. The Earth planted. This group corresponds in general to the work of the Second and Third Days (Gen. 1. 6–13).

Tablet V.—Creation and ordering of the Heavenly bodies. Corresponds nearest of all to the Fourth Day (Gen. 1. 14–19).

Tablet VI.—*Lost.*

Tablet VII.—Creation of Cattle and Creeping things, and probably Man also. Corresponds to the Sixth Day (Gen. 1. 24–31).

There are, however, some portions in the Assyrian tablets which appear to be displaced, and which we shall see, by being separately compared, render the resemblance to the Hebrew more close than appear at first sight.

In treating of the use which may be made of these tablets for comparative purposes, it will be better to deal first with those which relate strictly to the work of Creation, reserving until later any comments upon those of a more mythological character.

An examination of these documents, especially a comparison of the Assyrian and Babylonian versions, appears

## COMPARATIVE TABLE.

### First Tablet.

#### Assyrian Tablet.

1 At that time on high the heavens were un-named,
2 Below on the wide earth a name was not recorded.
3 The first-born Ocean was their generator.
4 The chaotic sea was the bearing mother of them all.
5 Their waters as one were folded together.
6 The cornfield was unharvested, the pasture had not sprung up.
7 When as yet the gods had not come forth any of them
8 A name was not recorded, order did not exist.
9 They were made even the great gods.
10 Lakhmu and Lakhamu came forth.
11 Until they spread . . . . .
12 Far extended were the days, until the gods An-Sar and Ki-Sar were made.
13 The god Anu.

### Hebrew Narrative.

#### Elohistic.

In the beginning God (*Elohim*) created the Heaven and the Earth.
And the Earth was waste and void, and darkness was upon the face of the deep (*Tehom*), and the spirit of God moved upon the face of the waters.

#### Jehovistic.

In the day when the LORD God (*Yahvek Elohim*) made Earth and Heavens,
No plant of the field was yet in the Earth, and no herb of the field had yet sprung up: for The Lord God had not caused it to rain upon the Earth, and there was not a man to till the ground. But there went up a mist from the Earth, and covered the whole face of the ground.

First Creation Tablet, copied about B.C. 660.
(*Photographed from the original.*)

to indicate that the series was compiled from the works of two schools of religious teaching, the Tablets II., III., and IV. being largely influenced by the ancient school of Eridu.

The great importance of this inscription—fragmentary as it is—will be at once recognised by Biblical students. It agrees in many points with the Hebrew records. In the general account of the chaotic state of nature with the Elohistic account, while in its more detailed features it approaches nearer to that of the Jehovistic writer. When, however, we proceed to examine and compare these stories of the world's birth, some remarkable differences will also be noticed.

The first Tablet may be said to form the opening verses of the Assyrian "Genesis," and was no doubt the basis of the account of Babylonian cosmological theories given by Damascios, a writer of the sixth century, he probably having obtained them from older, but now lost, works. "The Babylonians," he states, "like the rest of the barbarians, pass over in silence the one principle of the universe, and constitute two—Tavthê and Apason, making Apason the husband of Tavthê, and denominating her 'the mother of the gods.' From these proceed an only-begotten son, Mumis, which I conceive is no other than the intelligible world proceeding from the two principles. From them another progeny is derived, Dakhe and Dakhos; and, again, a third, Kissare and Assaros, from whom three others proceed, Anos, Illinos, and Aos; and of Aos and Davkê is born a son, called Belos, who they say is the fabricator of the world."

In the curious account of Babylonian cosmogony preserved by Berosos is found so little resemblance to the Hebrew that it hardly enters the field of comparison. So also in the tablet found at Kutha, the inscription to which we must assign to an old school of scribes.

The following Table will show how closely Damascios has followed the tablet :—

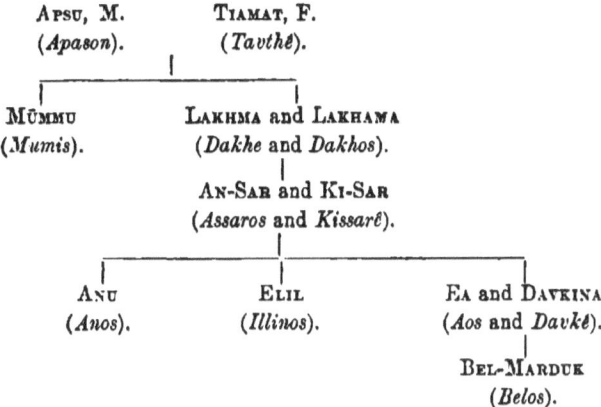

We see that both the Hebrew and the Assyrian accounts agree in representing the state of nature prior to the work of Creation as a chaotic mass, without order or arrangement.

## THE DIVINE WORD.

There is one curious point in regard to this pre-Creation period which brings the tablets into closer agreement with the Mosaic record than at first appears. "At the time when the Heavens above were un-named, below on the wide earth a name was not recorded." Here the use of the two verbal forms, *nabu*, "to proclaim," and *zakaru*, "to record," seems to point to the same idea of the Divine word being the power of Creation as in the Hebrew, "God said let there be light and there was light." This creative power of the Divine command is curiously illustrated by a tablet, containing a hymn to the Moon-god, in the British Museum (W. A. I., iv. 9) :—

> As for thee, thy word is declared and spreads on high as the wind: the stall and the fold are quickened.
> As for thee, thy will is established, and verdure is created.
> As for thee, thy will in the stall and cote is made known, and the seed of life is increased.

It will be seen that the creation of verdure, and the increase of flock and herd, is attributed to the declaration of the Divine command (*amat*). So that Heaven and Earth, being un-named, were not in existence.

*Tiamat.* This being corresponds exactly to the Tehom of Genesis, the watery waste which covered the surface, and is also to be identified with Tavthê, the wife of Apason, in the cosmogony of Damascios.

In the tablet she is called *Mūallidat*, "the bearing mother" of all the Heavens and Earth; and in the older legend from Kutha she is called *Musenik*, "the nutrice of them all." She is represented on the monuments as having the body of a woman, terminating in the coiled tails of two serpents, similar to the figures on the sculptures from Pergamos. In this form she represents the great nature-serpent of darkness, who coils round the earth like an egg, and holds the earth in its toils, until slain by Merodach, the Lord of Light.

As the personification of chaos and darkness, Tiamat becomes the Spirit of Evil, against whom Merodach, the god of goodness, the "protector of good men," wages eternal war.

*Lakhmu* and *Lakhamu.* It is difficult in the present state of our knowledge to clearly identify these characters. As in one of the mythological tablets we find them identified with Anu and Anatum, the Lord and Lady of Heaven, they may, perhaps, correspond to the firmament which divided the realms of nature.

*An-Sar* and *Ki-Sar*. These are two compound words, composed of An-Sar, "Heaven host," and Ki-Sar, "Earth host," they being the host of Heaven and Earth, the spirit forms which were afterwards known as the Annunaki and the Igigi, and who may be identified with the creations described in the passage, "Thus the Heavens and the Earth were finished, and all the host of them" (Gen. 2. 1). This expression, "*Zabaoth ha Šamaim*" of the Bible, becomes equivalent to the Assyrian expression *Kissat šamie*, "the Host of Heaven."

The great serpent of Chaos and Night having been slain, and the imprisoned earth released and divided from the heavens, the three great gods come forth to assume the government in their respective kingdoms.

1. *Anu* bears the titles of "Father of all the gods," The Progenitor who changes not the decrees coming forth from his mouth, The Mighty Chief, The Supreme, The Magnificent Lord of the Heaven, The Heaven.

2. *Ellu* or *Bel*. This deity, known as the Older Bel, to distinguish him from Bel Merodach, is the lord of the world; The lord who guards the country; Establisher of riches, wealth, and possessions; Lord of the mountain of the north (east), and described in Isaiah 14. Among his numerous titles one is of especial interest. In the hymns he is entitled *Ilu Sadu-rabu*, or *Ilu Sakū-rabu*, "The most high god," which Dr. Delitzsch has with great accuracy compared with the Biblical El Shaddai.

3. *Ea*, the Aos of Damascios. This is the most important god in the Babylonian pantheon, and although here only the third member of the great nature Trinity, is most frequently met with in the religious literature. The worship of Ea, the god of the Ocean, was undoubtedly the oldest cult in Babylonia, having as its centre the ancient City of Eridu or Eridugga, on the Persian Gulf. The "Holy City," as its name signifies, was the centre of a school of theologians who composed the most important works in the religious literature of Chaldea. These hymns, which M. Lenormant has so well described as the Rig-Veda of Chaldea, are of the most high character, and relate to the religion of Ea, "the all-wise god," and his son, the Sun-god Merodach, under his title of *Silik-mulu-dugga*, "the proctector of good men." Here Merodach appears as the Mediator between God and Man, and as the healer of Sickness and Sin.

The epithets applied to Ea are numerous: "Lord of the Sea," "Lord of the Ocean," "Lord of the House of Knowledge," "Lord of the Far-seeing Eye," "He who knows all things." The position occupied by Ea in the classical religious texts approaches very near to that of Jehovah in the Biblical narrative. He is the Creator of Man, the Protector of Shamas-Napisti, the Chaldean Noah, in the great danger of the Deluge.

Thus may be seen that Heaven, Earth, and the mysterious region of the under-world are now occupied by the divine rulers.

## The Fifth Tablet.

The Fifth Tablet is the largest of the strictly Creation Tablets, and is also the most important, as it presents striking agreements with the Biblical account, at the same time there are certain remarkable variations, which are of considerable interest in comparing the two accounts.

The tablet contains portions of about twenty-two lines of writing, but the reverse is not inscribed except with the endorsement: "Tablet V. (of the series), *Enu-va Elis.*"

The tablet, like the first of the series, comes from the royal library of Assurbanipal at Nineveh, but a Babylonian duplicate is also in the collection, coming from the temple-library at Sippara.

The translation of the document (see opposite page), together with the corresponding Biblical record, will show its great importance.

It presents a striking resemblance to the Hebrew account of the work of the Fourth Day (Gen. 1. 14–19), and is clear from the passage in line 8 that a Divine Creator is referred to, to whom the production of the heavenly bodies is due, and whose satisfaction is expressed in the words *ubassim*, "he made pleasant," which is a curious and striking parallel to the Hebrew refrain, "And God saw that it was good." As the two other members, Bel or Ellu and Ea, are here mentioned by name, it is evident that the Creator is the great "Heaven Father," Anu. It is he who establishes the position of the Stars and causes the Moon and the Sun to shine.

It should be noticed that there is a difference in the order of Creation in the tablet, and in the Hebrew record

## TRANSLATION.

### Assyrian Tablet.

1. He made pleasant the positions of the great gods.
2. The constellations* he arranged them, the double stars † he fixed.
3. He ordained the year, he appointed the Zodiac ‡ signs over it
4. The twelve months of constellations by threes he fixed
5. From the day when the year commenced to its close.
6. He established the position of the crossing stars § and for the seasons their bounds
7. Not to make fault or error of any kind.
8. The abode of Bel and Ea along with himself he fixed.
9. He opened great gates on either side
10. He bolts he made strong on the right hand and left
11. In the mass he made an ascent (staircase).
12. He Illuminator he cause to shine to rule the night.
13. He appointed him to establish the night until the coming forth of the day
14. (saying) Each month without fail by thy disk keep thou watch.
15. At the beginning of the month at the rising of the night.‖
16. Horns shine forth to announce the night.
17. On the seventh day to a disk it fills up.
18. Open thou and cause the rays of thy face to shine
19. At that time the Sun on the horizon of heaven at thy coming
20.     thou shalt divide the form
21.        towards the path of the Sun thou drawest near
23.         then the shining of the Sun shall change
24.           seeking his path
25.         set thou as by law decreed.

### Hebrew Narrative.

1. And God (*Elohim*) said, Let there be lights in the firmament of heaven to divide the day from the night, and let them be, for signs and for seasons, and for days and years: and let them be for lights in the firmament of heaven to give light upon the earth: and it was so. And God made the two great lights; the greater light to rule the day, and the lesser light to rule the night; he made the stars also. And God set them in the firmament of heaven to give light upon earth, and to rule over the day and over the night: And God saw that it was good.

---

* *Kakkabi*, "Groups of stars."

† *Lu Masi*, a particular set of seven double stars, called by Oppert the stars of the week.

‡ *Mizrata umazzir*: the *mizrata* were the *Mazzaroth* of Job 38. 22, by which the year was regulated.

§ *Nibiri*, from *ebiru*, "to cross"; literally, the "ferry boats."

‖ *Lillate*, "Twilight"; Hebrew, *Lilith*.

F

of the Fourth Day, which is of so marked a character as to call for comment.

ORDER OF CREATION.

If we tabulate the events as recorded according to their respective order, we see that the one is the direct opposite of the other.

| Assyrian Tablet. | Hebrew Narrative. |
|---|---|
| 1. The Stars, | 1. Sun. |
| 2. The Zodiac signs. | Day. |
| 3. The Four Seasons. | 2. The Moon. |
| 4. The Equinoxes and Solstices. | Night. |
| 5. The Night. | 3. Stars. |
| 6. The Month. | |
| 7. The Day, and Sun. | |

It will be seen that with the Assyrians, or rather, Babylonians, the stars come first in the order of the time measurers. It is their constellations that mark out the path of time, and divide the year into seasons.

In the Babylonian account it is evident that we have the work of a nation of astronomers proceeding under a regular established law of precedence in laying out the scheme of the heavenly bodies.

Taking the events in order, it will be seen how perfect their study of the heavenly bodies was, and how exactly the law of all time was regulated. The heavenly lights, according to the Biblical account, were created for signs and for seasons and for days and years, "and not to make fault or error of any kind," as the tablet states. This same astronomical regulation is explained by a tablet of the great royal observatory at Nineveh (W. A. I., iii. 53), which reads: "Twelve months for each year, 360 (60 × 6) days in number, are recorded. The rising and appearance of the moon one watches; the balancing of the stars and the moon, and their opposition to each other. For the year its months, for the month its days, the tale is complete. The twelve months in full, from beginning to end, to the measure of days fixed." This remarkable extract from a tablet written probably two thousand years before the Christian era, certainly shows the accurate nature of Babylonian astronomy.

"He ordained the years, and appointed the signs of the Zodiac over it." It requires but a very slight study of the Babylonian calendar to see that the months were named and arranged according to the signs of the Zodiac. This is best shown by the Table on the following page.

The division of the path of the sun through the heavens into the twelve divisions of the signs of the Zodiac must have been known in Babylonia at a very early period. It will be observed the names of the months, which correspond to the Zodiac signs, are those of the old Akkadian and not of the Semitic Calendar, which latter seem rather to be based upon the agricultural system, and in this respect corresponds to the old Hebrew Calendar.

It is evident that when the signs were first arranged, the opening constellation was that of the "propitious," or "directing bull"[*]—when the sun, as the "strong bull of Heaven," commenced to plough his straight furrow through the sky.

By the law of the precession of the equinoxes, we know that as far back as B.C. 2500 the sun's vernal equinox fell in

---

[*] See Sayce, *Hibbert Lectures*, p. 397.

## The Babylonian Calendar and the Zodiac.

| No. | Akkadian Month. | Sign. | Semitic Month. | Meaning. | Correspond. | Divine Regents. | Notes and Remarks. |
|---|---|---|---|---|---|---|---|
| 1. | Month of Holy Altar | Ram (*Aries.*) | Nisanno | Opening | Mar.-Apr. | Anu and Bel | Vernal Equinox. |
| 2. | ,, Propitious Bull | Bull (*Taurus.*) | Airu | Light | Apr.-May | Ea, the lord of Mankind. | |
| 3. | ,, making Bricks} ,, the Twins } | Twins (*Gemini.*) | Sivannu | Clay | May-June | Sin, the first-born son of Bel. | |
| 4. | ,, Fulness of Seed | Crab (*Cancer.*) | Duzu | Tammuz | June-July | Adar the Warrior | Summer Solstice. |
| 5. | ,, Fire makes Fire | Lion (*Leo.*) | Ab | - | July-Aug. | The Lady of the Wood of Life. | |
| 6. | ,, Message of Goddess. | Virgin (*Virgo.*) | Ulul | - | Aug.-Sept. | Istar, Lady of Battles. | |
| 7. | ,, Holy Mound | Claw of Scorpion. | Tasritu | The altar | Sept.-Oct. | Sun god, the warrior of all. | Autumnal Equinox. |
| 8. | ,, Laying Foundation. | Scorpion (*Scorpio.*) | Arakh samna. | Eighth month. | Oct.-Nov. | Merodach, counsellor of the gods. | |
| 9. | ,, Clouds | Archer (*Sagittarius.*) | Kislivu | Giant | Nov.-Dec. | Nergal the Hero. | |
| 10. | ,, Coming forth of Sea. | Goat (*Capricornus.*) | Dhebitu | Inundation | Dec.-Jan. | Papsukal, messenger of Ishar and Anu. | |
| 11. | ,, Curse of Rain | Water-carrier (*Aquarius.*) | Sebadhu | Destruction | Jan.-Feb. | Rimmon, the smiter of Heaven and Earth. | |
| 12. | ,, Sowing of Seed | Fish (*Pisces.*) | Adaru | Darkness | Feb.-Mar. | The seven great Gods | Winter Solstice. |

BOUNDARY STONE OF NEBUCHADNEZZAR I., B.C. 1120.
(*Photographed from the original.*)

Aries, so that the period when Taurus was the opening constellation must have been about B.C. 4700. It is evident from the gems and engraved stones, and especially from the curiously sculptured boundary stones, that prior to B.C. 2000 the constellations had been arranged in their present order. Considering, then, the great antiquity of this division of the sun's path, it is especially interesting to find the mention of the Mazzaroth or Zodiac signs in the Book of Job (**38**. 32), which many regard as one of the oldest works of Hebrew literature.

The names given to the signs appear in all probability to have been given in the old *totem* stage of the Akkadian people, and this seems to be confirmed by the fact that the divine regents of the months correspond to the signs of the Zodiac and the totem signs of the gods themselves. These totem signs are extremely old, and are preserved upon numerous boundary stones in the British and other museums.

### BOUNDARY STONE OF NEBUCHADNEZZAR I.

Upon this boundary stone, which, though a late example, is one of the best preserved, are most of the signs represented—the Ram, the Bull, Scorpion, the Saggitarius, together with many of the totem emblems of the gods.*

The path of the sun having been marked out and divided into twelve stations, these were again subdivided into four groups, divided from each other by fixed points. As we read in the tablet: "He fixed the place of the *Nibiri*, for the seasons their bounds." This passage is one of considerable interest, as the word *Nibiru* really means the

---

For further information see Lenormant, *Beginnings of History*, p. 240.

ferry-boat, and the divine ferry-boat was chiefly associated with Merodach, who is called *Ilu Nibiru*, "the god of the ferry-boat"—doubtless in his capacity as the lord of the solar bark, like the boat of Ra in the mythology of Egypt.\* In the month Tasritu—the autumn month—he is especially so called, because in this month the sun is ferried over from one half of the year to the other. The Nibiri here must certainly mean the constellations which mark the points on the circle when the sun passes from one division of the year to the other, and this seems to be confirmed by a very valuable inscription, still unpublished, which gives us the seasons of the year as observed in Babylonia.†

The first portion of the tablet is lost, but the text can be easily restored :—

### TABLET OF SEASONS.

1st Season (lost)—From the 1st day of Adar (Feb.–March) to the 30th day of Airu (April–May), the season of rain and sunshine. The latter rain of the Jewish Calendar.

2nd Season—" From the 1st day of Sivan (May–June) to the 30th day of Ab (July–Aug.), the Sun is in the course of Bel, the season of crops and fruit." This was the wheat harvest and fruit season in Palestine.

3rd Season—" From the 1st day of Elul (Aug.–Sept.) to the 30th day of Marchesvan (Oct.–Nov.), the Sun is in the course of Anu, the season of rain and clouds."

---

\* Compare the Zodiac of Denderah, which is, however, of late date, probably about A.D. 42.

† Tablet marked S 1,907 in British Museum.

FESTIVALS OF THE SUN-GOD. 55

This was the period of the former or autumn rain in Palestine.

4th Season—"From the 1st day of Kislevu (Nov.-Dec.) to the 30th day of Sebat (Jan.-Feb.), the Sun is in the course of Ea, the season of storms." This is the winter season of Palestine.

It will be observed from this inscription that the four points on the ecliptic or sun's path fall almost in the centre of each season and not at the commencement, and this leads to the conclusion that the Nibiri were the constellations marking the equinoxes and solstices; this conjecture seems to be substantiated by the valuable list of solar festivals found in the tablet of Nabu-apla-iddina, king of Babylon, who reigned about B.C. 900. In this tablet, now in the British Museum,\* the king mentions the festivals of the Sun-god, which were celebrated at Sippara in his time. The dates of these are very important':—

1. Month Nisan, 7th day.
2. Month Airu, 10th day.†
3. Month Elul, 3rd day.
4. Month Tisritu, 7th day.
5. Month Marchesvan, 15th day.†
6. Month Adar, 15th day.‡

Two of these dates are extremely important, namely, those of the 7th of Nisan and the 7th of Tisri, because they correspond most closely to the Hebrew festivals of the Passover on the 15th of Nisan, and the Day of Atonement,

---

\* Printed in W. A. I., v. 60, 61. For illustration see frontispiece. In succeeding pages W. A. I. stands for cuneiform inscriptions of Western Asia, published by the Trustees of the British Museum.

† These seem to me to be old equinoxial festivals which have been passed over in the course of the precession of the equinoxes.

‡ Perhaps the origin of the Jewish Feast of Purim. There was a festival near the end of the year, when the gods met in solemn conclave to decide the destinies of all men during the coming year, but its exact date is not known.

which was kept on the 10th day of Tisri (Lev. 16), and both of these festivals correspond very closely with the vernal and autumnal equinoxes.

With these facts before us, I am inclined to think that the *Nibiri* were the equinoxes and, possibly, the solstices as well. We know, from the inscriptions, that the Assyrians and Babylonians very carefully watched for these important periods, this is proved by the reports of astronomers in the library of Nineveh. Thus in one report we read, "Month Nisan, 6th day,* the day and the night were balanced. Six *kaspu*† day, six *kaspu* night. May Nebo and Merodach to the king, my lord, be propitious." In another report from the same library we read, "Month Nisan, 15th day, the day and the night were balanced. Six *kaspu* day, six *kaspu* night." Here, then, is a variation of nine days in the fall of the vernal equinox, but it is evident that it was closely and attentively watched for.

One other festival remains, which may also have been one of the *Nibiri*, namely, the great festival on the 1st day of Nisan, the Feast of the New Year. This was a day of very great importance, for from it the king dated the years of his reign. Between the death of a former king and the 1st of Nisan his successor always dated his tablets *ina satti ris sarrutu*, "in the year of the beginning of royalty" (2 Kings 25. 27).

On the evening of the same day was celebrated the great festival of Bel Merodach, the ritual of which is preserved to us, and presents a curious resemblance to that observed by the Jewish High Priest on the Day of Atonement (Lev. 16. 14).

---

* W. A. I., vol. i., pl. 51-53.   † A period of "two hours."

"In the month Nisan, on the 2nd day* in the first *kaspu* of the evening, the priest shall come, and draw of the waters of the river, and entering into the presence of Bel the veil † he sprinkles, and to Bel he shall say this prayer."

The prayer, which is one of the most beautiful in the liturgy of the great temple of Babylon, will be dealt with subsequently.

Although the monuments as yet have afforded no evidence of it, there was probably a similar festival on the 1st of Tasritu, corresponding to the Jewish Feast of Trumpets, or the *Rosh Ha-shana*, "New year" (Lev. 23. 24, 25).

From the foregoing it may be concluded that the *Nibiri* were certain fixed points which the sun crossed in its course, and the times of its doing so were observed as festivals. It is also apparent that in the Babylonian teaching, as in the Hebrew, the celestial bodies were created to be time measures, "not to make fault or error of any kind." The orbit seems to have been divided among the great gods, and the reference in line eight is explained by the tablet of the seasons already quoted.

## Moon Worship.

We now come to the most valuable portion of this tablet, which enables us to make some interesting comparisons with the Hebrew story. It will be observed that the next work of creation, that of the Moon, is assigned a priority over the sun, whereas in the Hebrew account this order is reversed, namely, "the greater light to rule the day,

---

\* This would be after sunset on the 1st, the Babylonian day, like that of the Jews, beginning at sunset.
† The words mean literally "the hanging cloth."

and the lesser light to rule the night"; this difference, apparently small, is of very great importance, as it affords information as to the source of the traditions.

The essential differences which exist between the agriculturist and the nomad in their mode of life, the one being in every respect the very antithesis of the other, must naturally find a repetition in religion. We meet with this at the very threshold of Hebrew history in the different methods adopted by Cain and Abel in approaching their God. Cain, the agriculturist, the settler, brings his offering, "the fruit of the ground"; but Abel, the nomad, brings the acceptable offering, the "firstlings of the flock, and of the fat thereof" (Gen. 4. 3, 4). The same rivalry repeats itself in the story of Esau and Jacob. In Arab life, where the true nomad spirit so long survived, and is not yet entirely obliterated, the same rivalry exists. The sayings of Mohammed, traditional though they may be, reflect this contrast : *e.g.* "The Divine Glory" (*al Sakinat*), he said, "is among the shepherds; vanity and impudence among the agriculturists."\* And again, on seeing a ploughshare and another agricultural implement, he said, "These implements do not enter into the house of a nation, unless that impudence enter in there at the same time"; and this is further endorsed in the political testament of the Chalif Omar, who says to his successor, "Protect the Bedawi, for they are the root of the Arabs and the germ of Islam."†

This contrast repeats itself in religious as also in social life. The nomad loves his flocks and herds; his wealth depends upon the quality of the pasturage he can get

---

\* Goldziher, *Mythology of the Hebrews*, p. 81.   † *Ibid.*, p. 82.

for them; and to seek this he leads an ever-roving life. How beautifully this feeling is expressed by the Hebrew Psalmist (23. 1, 2), "The LORD is my shepherd; I shall not want. He maketh me to lie down in green pastures: he leadeth me beside the still waters." The cloudy sky, which sends rain* and dew, is his friend, while the hot burning sun, which scorches up his pastures and drinks up the streams, is to him a foe. Neither is this love of the moist water-giving night absent from the Hebrew mind, as seen in the blessing of Isaac (Gen. 27. 28)—"And God give thee of the dew of heaven, and the fatness of the earth, and plenty of corn and wine." So also notice the contrast between the terrible heat of harvest and the cool refreshing dew in the passage, "like a cloud of dew in the heat of harvest" (Isa. 18. 4).

Turning now to the inscriptions, we see the same contrast preserved, and the love of the moon and the night clearly indicated as one of the features of Semitic Babylonian life; this idea is predominant in a beautiful hymn, which has, fortunately, been preserved in a very perfect state; it has an increased value to Biblical students as coming from the liturgy of the temple of Ur of the Chaldees. I do not translate the whole of it, as portions have no direct bearing on the subject.†

### HYMN TO MOON-GOD.
*Translation.*

Strong ox, whose horns are mighty, whose limbs are seemly, whose beard is crystal;
Offspring who by himself is created, his eye is full of adornment.

---

\* 1 Kings 18. 44, 45.
† The hymn is published in W. A. I., iv. 9, and a complete translation will be found in Sayce's *Hibbert Lectures*, pp. 159, 160.

Merciful one, begetter of the universe, who among the living creatures raises his holy abode.

Father, long-suffering and forgiving, who all living things upholds by his hand;

Oh, Lord, thy divinity, like the far distant heavens and the wide spread sea, fills all (with) fear.

On the peopled earth he places his holy places, and proclaims their names.

Oh, Father, begetter of gods and men, who causes the abode to be raised, who establishes the free-will offering,

Who proclaims sovereignty, giving the sceptre—who knows the destiny unto a far remote day.

Firstborn omnipotent, whose heart unfathomable, none can know.

(*Some lines too broken.*)

In Heaven who is supreme? Thou alone art supreme!

On earth who is supreme? Thou alone art supreme!

As for thee, thy word is proclaimed in heaven, and the angels bow down their faces.

As for thee, thy word is proclaimed on earth, and the spirits of earth kiss the ground.

As for thee, thy word is spread on high like the wind, and stall and fold are quickened.

As for thee, thy word on earth is established, and verdure is created.

As for thee, thy word in stall and sheep-cote becomes visible, and living creatures are increased.

As for thee, thy word has brought forth law and justice, so that mankind has established a law.

As for thee, thy word (is as) the far distant heavens and the deep buried earth, none can know it.

As for thee (and) thy word, who shall learn it? who shall repeat it?

Oh, Lord, in heaven is thy lordship, on earth is thy dominion.

Among the gods, thy brethren, a rival thou hast not.

This ancient hymn, probably older than the time of Abraham, is a true desert chant, redolent of the sheep-cote and cattle-pen. The Moon, the Lord of the Night, is giver of everything that benefits man, and, above all, of the precious rain, as in the earlier part of the text we find this beautiful passage, "Thou holdest the lightning, protector of all living things, there is no god who hath at any time discovered thy fulness." This exactly expresses the same thoughts as the passages from Hebrew and Arabic writers already mentioned. It will be seen why in documents such as these, essentially Semitic in thought, the Moon takes the priority of the Sun. It was so in the days of the Chaldeans' nomad life, it remained so for centuries after they had become settled in Babylonia. There was but one great centre of Moon-worship in Babylonia, and this, strangely enough, the city which we may regard as the birth-place of the Hebrew nation, namely, Ur of the Chaldees, the Moon being called "Lord of Ur"; but there were numerous shrines of the Sun-god, indeed, every city had its local Sun-god or solar hero.

The Sun in ancient mythology is always closely associated with agriculture, trade, and with city life. This may be illustrated by some extracts from a remarkable hymn to the Sun :—

### Hymn to the Sun-God.

In the day of raising shouts, and boasting, and pleasures,
Approach, oh, Shining One! Their wine, their drink, they pour
    out for thee—a noble drink, thou acceptest it!
Their shining and bright drink offerings thou acceptest, thou
    drinkest their *mizi* wine.
The plans they ponder upon, thou makest to succeed;
Those that are borne down, their ban thou dost loose;
Those that pray, thou acceptest their prayers;
They also fearing thee, preserve thy renown.

   \*    \*    \*    \*    \*    \*    \*

What hills are there that are not clothed with thy splendour?
What regions are there which are not warm with the brightness
  of thy light?
Thou that drivest away obscurity, that makest light the darkness,
That openest the darkness, that makest bright the wide earth.

The Sun in this mythology is essentially the god of the day and of the affairs of the day; its connection with the laws of men is of a far more concrete character than that attributed to the Moon-god in the hymn already quoted. The Sun-god in Babylonia, like the Greek Helios, was ever the all-seeing judge of men, as will be seen in the following lines :—

The unjust judge, thou showest him bonds;
He who takes bribes, who is not rightly guided, upon him thou
  puttest sin;
But he who accepts not a bribe, that takes the part of the weak,
Good things in life from Shamas shall he profit.
The wise judge, who gives a righteous judgment, he shall attain
  the palace, the abode of nobles his dwelling.

The priority of the Moon over the Sun is again expressed when the goddess Istar speaks of the Moon-god as her father and of the Sun as her brother. In the beautiful prayer of Assur-nazir-pal I., already quoted in another chapter, the goddess Istar is addressed as: "The daughter of the Moon, the sister of the Sun-god."

This reversal of the order of the creation of the heavenly bodies in the Babylonian, as compared with the Hebrew, affords a direct contrast between the two, and precludes the theory of direct copying. In addition, it seems strongly to show that the Hebrew version, in the present form, must have been compiled at a period when the old traditions and love of nomad life had grown faint.

THE GATES OF THE SUN. 63

As natural in a work the product of a people learned in astronomy, and subject to the influence of learned neighbours, the Babylonian account presents a more detailed account of the work of creation than that of the Hebrew writer.

"He opened great gates in the side of the world." The conception that the heavenly bodies made their entrance and exit from the regions below through great gates is one common to most ancient mythologies. In the Egyptian Ritual of the Dead we have the fifteen great pylons of Karneter, guarded by genii, armed with swords, through which the deceased had to pass, and through which Osiris passed daily. This idea appears to have survived in the Book of Enoch, where the sun rises and sets through great gates. These gates are very fully described in a portion of the Epic of Gilgames (Tablet ix., col. ii.),* where we read, "To the mountains whose form is double. To the double mountains in his course he came, which each day guard the Sun. Above them is the threshold of heaven; below them the house of death embraces them. Scorpion men, they guard the great gate, whose terror is terrible and their beholding death."—Through these great gates then, rise the Moon and the Sun.

The Moon-god is here called by the name which seems more especially his name in the worship in the temple of Ur, the city of Abram. This name of *Nannaru* is a corruption of *Namnaru*, "the Illuminator," and is evidently the name which gave rise to the curious myth of Nannaros, a Persian legend preserved by Ctesias;† it is particularly

---

* See my translation with full text, *Babylonian and Oriental Record*, vol. iii., p. 90.
† See Dunker, *History of Antiquity*, v., p. 298.

interesting, for it was the local title of the Moon-god, not only in Ur, where he is addressed as *Abu Nannar belum ilu dhabu ebili ilani*, "Father Nannar, Lord and good god, ruling the gods," but also in the city of Kharran, which is so closely associated with Ur in the Scriptural narrative (Gen. 11. 31). Nabonidus addresses the Moon-god of Kharran by the title of *Nannari samie u irzitum*, "Illuminator of Heaven and Earth." In the hymn from the Liturgy of Ur, already referred to, the Akkadian equivalent is *Ur + Ki* or *Sis + Ki*, "Light of the Earth," and the temple of the god was called "the House of the great light."

## The Name of Sinai.

Another name of the Moon-god was that of Sin. This name is found only in Assyria, Babylonia, and on the coasts of Arabia, but the etymology of the name is still obscure. It is, however, important to notice that his name is closely associated with the land of Magan, or the peninsula of Sinai, and there may be, as Professor Sayce has suggested, a connection between the name of the Holy Mountain, and that of the old Semitic Moon-god. In connection with this interesting subject, upon which as yet there is too little evidence, may be noticed that one of the most common epithets of the Moon-god Sin was that of *Bel terite*, "Lord of laws," and is called in the Hymn from Ur, "he who has created law and justice, so that mankind has established law," and again, "the ordainer of the laws of heaven and earth."

If Sinai in these remote ages, centuries before the time of Moses, was so closely associated with the "Lord of the laws," may it not throw some light on its selection as the Mountain of the Law by the Mosaic writers.*

The Moon was called by the Akkadians by the name of En-Zu, "the Lord of Waxing and Waning," and this name seems to have been almost purely of an astronomical or cosmical character. A third name, apparently of foreign origin, was that of Agu or Aku, "the disk."

## "The Month."

The tablet then proceeds to describe the phases of the Moon, with that fulness of detail which we should expect from so astronomical a race as the Babylonians. "Every month without fail its disk he appointed." It is evident, therefore, that among the Babylonians, as among the Hebrews, the observance of the New Moon, which appeared at "the rising of the night," was a matter of great importance.

That a careful watch was kept is shown by the reports in the astronomical libraries of Assyria. A number of these reports are in the British Museum (W. A. I., vol. iii., pl. 51, Nos. 3, 4, 5, 6). "A watch we kept; on the 29th day the Moon we see. May Nebo and Merodach to the King, my Lord, draw near. Report of Nabu of (the city) of Assur." Those who have travelled in the East have not failed to notice how keen is the sight of these sons of the desert to catch the first thin line of the crescent. As with the Jews of old watching for the Paschal Moon, so with the followers of Islam for the Moon of Ramazan. In Assyria

---

* The word *teriti* is the plural of *tertu*, "a law," which is the exact equivalent of the Hebrew *torah*, and one of the most important officials in Babylon was the *bel tertu*, "Master of the Law."

H

also this watch was one of weary waiting, as shown by the following tablet dating B.C. 649 :—

> To the King, my Lord: Thy servant Istar-iddina-apla,
> One of the chief of the astronomers of Arbela.
> May there be peace to the King, my Lord;
> May Nebo, Merodach, and Istar of Arbela,
> To the King, my Lord, draw near.
> On the 29th day a watch we kept;
> The house of observation was covered with cloud;
> The Moon we did not see.
> Month Sebat (Jan.-Feb.), 1st day in the Eponym of Bel-Kharran-Sadua.

That not only the New Moon, but all the subsequent phases of the orb, were observed with care is shown by the tablet, "On the 7th day to a circle it approaches." The careful observation of the Moon is confirmed by another valuable astronomical tablet.*

> The Moon, on its appearance, from the 1st day to the 5th day
> For five days is visible. The Moon is Anu.
> From the 6th day to the 10th day for five days it is full
> (increasing). It is Ea.
> From the 11th day to the 15th day for five days to a crown
> it grows.
> The Moon is Anu Bel and Ea in its mass.

This seems to give the same divisions of the lunar orbit as those in line eight of the tablet, but it will be seen that they do not correspond to the true lunations. That these divisions so observed by the Hebrews and the Arabs were also observed by the Babylonians is demonstrated by more than one record of the past.

The bases of Babylonian cosmic calculation seem to have been those of the week, the month, and the year, and in the religious calendar the hebdominal groups predominated.

---

* W. A. I., iii. 55. 3.

## The Sabbath.

Among the most valuable treasures of the British Museum are important Sacred Calendars of the months Nisan, Elul, &c., which proves very clearly the knowledge and observance of the Sabbath. In these important documents we read that the 7th, 14th, 21st, 28th, also 19th days of the month were called *Udu khulgal,* an "unlawful day," *dies nefastus,* which is rendered also in a bilingual list (W. A. I., iii., 56. 53) by *Salum,* "rest or completion." Still more interesting is the valuable gloss in a lexicographical tablet (W. A. I., ii., 32. 16), where is found the word *Sabattum,* "the Sabbath," explained by the words *Yum nukh libbi,* "The day of the rest of the heart."

In another list the word *Sabbatu* is a synonym of *gamaru* "to complete, to finish."

In these Calendars we read the prescript:—

The seventh day is a resting day to Merodach and Zarpanit, a holy day, a Sabbath. The shepherd of mighty nations must not eat flesh cooked at the fire or in the smoke. His clothes he changes not. A washing he must not make. He must not offer sacrifice. The King must not drive in his chariot. He must not issue royal decrees. In a secret place the augur a muttering makes not. Medicine for the sickness of his body one must not apply. For making a curse it is not fit. In the night the King makes his free-will offering before Merodach and Istar. Sacrifice he slays. The lifting of his hand finds favour with his god.

The examination of these inscriptions, relating to the Sabbath among the Babylonians shows how exactly it fulfilled the words of the Hebrew writer, " On the seventh day God *finished* his work which he had made; and he *rested* on the seventh day from all his work which he had made. And God blessed the seventh day, and hallowed it:

because that in it he rested from all his work, which God had created and made" (Gen. 2. 2, 3).

The Sabbaths of the Babylonian Calendar do not appear to have been dedicated to any particular god, but rather to have embraced most of the pantheon.

Thus we find—

The 7th day was the holy day of Merodach and Ziratpanit.
The 14th, the holy day of Belel and Nergal.
The 21st, of the Moon and Sun.
The 28th, to the god Ea.

There are several points of great interest connected with this Babylonian Sabbath when compared with the Jewish; notice how strict were the observances: no work was to be done, no fire was to be lit for the cooking of food. The most interesting restriction is that which reads, *Asu ana marzu-su zumri ul uppal*, "medicine to the sickness of body he applies not," which seems to give the restriction which the Pharisees implied in the question to Jesus—" Is it lawful to heal on the Sabbath day?" (Matt. 12. 10.) Another interesting side-light on Jewish customs is that of the statement that the sacrifice must be offered in the evening or night (*musi*), the Sabbath having ended at sunset. It was for the same reason, no doubt, that the sick were brought to Christ after sunset (Mark 1. 32). There is, however, an additional matter of interest in this inscription which constitutes another close parallel with Hebrew sacred legislation. In the Calendar, the 19th day of the month is observed as a 'Sabbath. The reason for this is apparent when it is remembered that the 19th day of the month is the 49th, or seventh week, from the *first* of the previous month, thus constituting a Sabbatical week—the Feast of Weeks

(Deut. 16. 9–16). The Babylonians also observed the Sabbatical month in the particularly holy character of the month *Tasritum*, and apparently the Sabbatical year (Lev. 25. 3–8) in the *Karu* or cycle mentioned in the Eponyme Canon and on the Obelisk of Shalmaneser III.

## THE SUN AND DAY.

The portion of the tablet relating to the creation of the Sun is so mutilated that it will call for little comment. The path of the Sun-god is here called by the name of *Kharran Samsi*, "the road of the Sun." The Sun was regarded in Babylonian mythology as the "child of the Moon," reasons for which have already been explained. The chief centre of solar worship in Babylonia was the city of Sippara, or rather that quarter of the city known as the Sippara of the Sun-god.* Here was the great temple known as *E Barbara*, "the House of light," which, according to tradition, had existed before the Deluge, but which, at any rate, was an ancient edifice in as remote a period as B.C. 3800. As I shall have occasion to refer very fully to the services and ceremonies of this temple in a subsequent chapter, it will be sufficient to note one extract from a hymn to show the nature of the solar cultus of Babylonia :—

> Oh, Lord, illuminator of the darkness, opener of the face (of the sky);
> Merciful god, who setteth up the fallen, who keepeth the weak,
> Unto thy light turn the great gods.
> The spirits of Earth gaze towards thy face;
> The tongues of the host as one cry thou directest.
> Smiling, their heads they look to the light of the Sun.

---

* See Professor Sayce's remarks on the Sipparas, the Sepharvaim of the Bible (2 Kings 18), in his *Hibbert Lectures*, p. 169.

Like a wife art thou—glad, and making glad.*
Thou art the light in the vault of the far-off heaven ;
Thou art the eye-centre of all the wide spread lands ;
Men far and near behold thee and rejoice.
The great gods smelt the sweet savour, † the food of the
 shining heavens.
He who has not turned his hand to sin thou wilt prosper ;
He shall eat of thy food and be blessed by thee.

## CREATION OF MAN AND ANIMALS.

The next tablet is also very much mutilated. It corresponds to the work of the Sixth day in the Hebrew account (Gen. 1. 24, 25), the creation of the cattle and creeping things :—

When the gods in their assembly had created (great beasts)
They made perfect the mighty monsters ;
They caused the living creatures to come forth ;
The cattle of the field, the wild beasts of the field, and the creep-
 ing things of the field.
. . . . . . . . for the living creatures.
The cattle and creeping things of the city they sent forth ;
The assembly of creeping things and all the creation,
. . . . . . which is the assembly of my family.
Ea, the Lord of the illustrious face, the multitude of creeping
 things he made strong.

This small fragment bears a strong resemblance to the Hebrew version, and seems certainly to be the work of the same school as the writers of the fifth tablet of the series, it exhibits the same careful distinctions in detail.

---

* Here the Sun is regarded as feminine, a conception very common in mythologies, where lunar worship has preceded solar. This feminine conception of the Sun is not unknown to Hebrew, as in Gen. 15. 17. It will be observed that this phrase bears a direct contrast to that in Ps. 19. 5.

† Compare the expression "the Lord smelled the sweet savour" (Gen. 19. 21) and the extensive use of the phrase in regard to sacrifices in the Books of Leviticus and Deuteronomy. See also Col. III., 49, of the Deluge Tablet, "The gods smelled the odour, the gods smelled the sweet odour."

The expression *siknat napisti* is one of frequent occurrence in the inscriptions, and corresponds exactly to that in the Hebrew (Gen. 1. 24). There is a careful distinction made between the cattle—*pulu*—and the *umâam* or great wild beasts, and the latter word is omitted when the cattle of the city are mentioned.

The use of this word *umdam* for great wild beasts is of considerable interest; *e.g.*, it is used again in the hunting inscriptions of Tiglath-pileser I. (B.C. 1150), where we read "the rest of the numerous animals (*umáam*), winged birds of the air, which are among the beasts of the field."

In the same inscriptions the expression occurs, *umami sâ tiamtu*, "great beasts of the sea," which may certainly be compared with the *behemoth* of the Hebrew text.

It is very unfortunate that the lower portion of this tablet is so mutilated, as, had it been more perfect, it seems very probable that we should have had here the Babylonian version of the creation of man. The deity mentioned under the name of *Bel-eni-ellute*, "the Lord of the holy eye or countenance," is the god Ea, to whom most of the inscriptions assign the creation of the human race. In a tablet, which was at first regarded as the Babylonian story of the Fall, but which is now proved to be a hymn to Ea, the following passage occurs: *Ana padi-sunu ibnu avilutu Riminū sa bulludhu basū itte su*—"For their redemption did he create mankind, even he, the merciful one, with whom is life"; and in another fragment are the words, "Mayest thou be great, for a noble companion art thou. Let thy manhood be increased. With the dominion of all the gods I have caused thy hand to be filled," which, if it applies, as I think it does, to the creation of man, seems to be a remarkable parallel to the Hebrew, "Let us make man in our own image." In the same hymn we read, "May his word (*amatu*) be established, and not be forgotten in the mouth of mankind (*zalmat kakkadi*), whom his hands have created." Again, Merodach, in his character as the son of Ea, occupies a position but slightly inferior to that of his father, repeatedly assuming the divine epithets of his father; and in a hymn to Merodach, *Avilutum zalmat kakkadi siknat napisti mala suma nabu ina matati basa*—"Mankind (even), the human race, the living creatures, all that by name are called, and in the land exist, is thine." It would appear, therefore, that to Ea and Merodach, or the pair conjointly, that the Babylonians attributed the creation of the human race.*

It would seem also from a passage in a magical text of considerable antiquity, being certainly of Akkadian origin, that the story of the creation of woman from the rib of the man was known to the Babylonians, for we read, *Assat ina udli nis uttam,* " the woman from the flank of the man was called "—certainly this is a curious parallel to Gen. 2, 21, 22.

We have now completed our examination of these very important documents from the buried libraries of Babylonia and Assyria, and there remains still the difficult question of their date and relationship to the Hebrew version to be discussed.

Upon this important subject much valuable light has been thrown during the last few years by the discoveries in Babylonia. It was at one time the opinion of many scholars that the versions of these tablets, first published by Mr. George Smith, were of Assyrian origin, and, therefore, not of

---

* I shall treat more fully of this in the study of an older Creation Tablet at the end of this chapter.

earlier date than the time of Assur-bani-pal, about B.C. 650, and that, under these circumstances, Jewish influence might have been exercised in their composition. The discovery, however, of larger portions of these texts in the great library of the University Temple of Nebo at Borsippa removes this objection. This library was one of the oldest in Babylonia, being certainly in existence as early as B.C. 2500, as both the temple and the scribes of the temple are mentioned. The temple of Nebo, the Prophet-god, was the great centre of religious teaching in Babylonia, and was called "the House of Life"—the House of Knowledge. Here all the great religious texts were preserved and studied, and we have from its shelves duplicates of many well-known inscriptions of which we had already obtained copies from the library at Nineveh. Among these may be mentioned the Deluge Tablet, the War in Heaven, portions of the Gilgames Legends, and many grammatical texts. The valuable duplicate of the first Creation Tablet bears the following colophon or endorsement:—"Like its old copy, written and explained. The tablet of Nabu-balat-su-ikbi, son of . . . . who is not the Nabu-balat-su-ikbi, son of Naid-Marduk." In the duplicate of the fourth tablet a similar definite statement is made :—"Copied for Nebo by his lord, Naid-Marduk, the son of the irrigator, for the preservation of his life and the life of his house. He wrote and placed it in E-zida." It is evident from these statements that the documents were regarded as sacred texts, and placed by pious donors in the temples, like the gifts of a Missal or a Qūran by a pious Christian or Mohammedan. The construction of the Gilgames Epic shows that it must have been compiled as early as B.C. 2500–2200, probably during the great literary period under Khammu-rabi. In this we have the Deluge

I

story, and a description, as I shall show, of Eden and the Kerubim. We may, therefore, very reasonably suppose that these legends of the cosmogony were committed to literary form about this period.

Other arguments in favour of this conclusion may be found in the facts that the arrangements, names, and epithets of the gods in the inscriptions of this period are in strict accordance with the theogony of the Creation Tablets.

I have already pointed out that the prominence given to the Moon and Stars over the Sun, the reversal of the order of the Hebrew account in the fifth tablet, and the distinction between animals of town and country in the seventh tablet, marks the retention of the modes of thought of nomadic life in the minds of the compilers of these tablets, while the simple story of the Hebrew bears traces of the work of a thoughtful settled literary class.

It seems to me, upon the evidence shown in a former chapter of the long settlement of the Semites in Babylonia prior to the migration of Abram, that these traditions, at least perhaps in a simpler form, must have been known in Chaldea if not in other parts of Western Asia.

That there was a close literary intercourse between Egypt, Chaldea, and Palestine at an early date is now beyond doubt. In the year 1887 there were discovered at Tel el-Amarna, in Egypt, a number of documents—inscribed clay tablets—written in the cuneiform character, which supply the material for an almost complete reconsideration of many of the arguments formerly used as to the relation of the Babylonian and Hebrew primitive traditions. These tablets could only belong to one period, the time of the reigns of Amenophis III. and his son the heretic king Khu-en-Aten, that is, from about B.C. 1450-1500. An

TABLETS FROM TEL EL-AMARNA, B.C. 1450.
(*Photographed from the original.*)

examination of the tablets proved this to be the case, and the documents to be letters and despatches written to the kings of Egypt by the princes of Babylon—Mitani (North Mesopotamia) and other states. They proved that in the fifteenth century, that is, nearly two hundred years before the Exodus and the age of Moses, the cuneiform writing was the script of diplomacy in use in the principal states of Western Asia and at the court of the kings of Egypt. This is a very astonishing discovery, necessitating a very careful consideration in our attempt to establish a time relationship between the Hebrew and primitive Babylonian legends. There is, however, a still more important feature, and one which brings this evidence still more directly into the plane of argument. Many of these letters were from the towns of Canaan, from the cities of the Philistines, Amorites, and Phœnicians, showing that throughout the whole of the land, occupied some years later by the Israelites, the teaching of Babylonian scribes was established. There are letters from Askelon, Gaza, Lacish, Hazor, from Amorite princes, and from Jerusalem, thus proving that there were men in these towns able to read and write the Babylonian characters. If they could write they could read, and as they could read, the literature of Babylonia was accessible to them.

Among the tablets found at Tel el-Amarna were some not exclusively diplomatic, but literary tablets. Two of these are fairly perfect—the legend of Eris-Kigal, or the Babylonian Persephone, and the legend of "Adapa the Fisherman." There is also a hymn to the war god. This latter is the most important, as it contains an endorsement stating that it was a copy made in the library of Nebo at Borsippa, which tends to prove that library to have been in a flourishing condition as early as B.C. 1500. It is from this library that the greater number of our Creation and Deluge Tablets originally came.

Documents from this temple were studied in Egypt before the days of Moses, and scribes from this and other libraries taught the cuneiform writing to the scribes of Canaan. May not the traditions, which had been known to Abram five hundred or more years before, have been among those that were known to the learned at this time, and have formed the ground-work of Hebrew tradition? As already stated, there is a marked difference in many ways between the Hebrew and the later Chaldean reports, and which materially argues against a borrowing in the age of the Captivity.

That there was in post Captivity times a revision and a re-editing, I think most students will admit; but the Tel el-Amarna tablets have shown clearly that there was a possibility of these stories in some primitive form being known to the people of Canaan, and to the learned in Egypt, at least a century and a half before the days of Moses. To what extent this opportunity was used we know not as yet, but further research will no doubt reveal much to us. One important point is clear, that there is now introduced into the field of Biblical criticism, already crowded, a factor, and a powerful one, hitherto unknown, namely, the influence of a pre-Israelite Canaanite civilisation of a high standard, and in close and literary communication with Babylonia.

OLDER CREATION LEGENDS.

In a land with so many different religious centres and temple schools, each with its own systems of theology, it is natural that there would grow up various legends of the Creation. It is difficult to say to which school the tablets already considered belong, but in all probability they may be assigned to the priesthood of the great temple of Nebo at Borsippa. There are, however, in the British Museum, portions of tablets which fulfil our expectations as regards there being other and local legends of cosmogonic teaching. Two of these are of especial interest, as they both belong to an early period of religious development, namely, to the age when the old religio-magical creed had not been entirely replaced by a polytheistic creed.

## The Legend of Eridu.

A small tablet of grey clay written in Babylonian characters; it was first deciphered by Mr. T. G. Pinches, of the British Museum. The inscription is a bilingual, written in Akkadian and Semitic Babylonian, and is evidently a document belonging to the library of the great temple of Nebo at Borsippa. It is, however, as I shall shortly show, manifestly a product of an older school than that of Borsippa, and abounds in curious and interesting mythological details. I translate it as follows :—

> The holy house, the house of the gods, in a holy site had not been made.
> A reed had not sprung up, a tree was not made.
> A brick was not laid, a beam was not made.
> A house was not constructed, a city was not built.
> A city was not made, an abode was not made strong.
> Nipur had not been built, E Kurra was not constructed,
> Uruki had not been built, E Anna was not constructed.
> The Absu was not made. Eridu was not built.
> The holy house, the house of the gods, its site was not made.
> The whole world, the sea also
> In the midst of the sea was a flowing (tide).

## BEL MERODACH AS THE CREATOR.

At that time Eridu was built, E Sagila was constructed.
E Sagila which the god Lugal-du-azagga within the Absu raised up.
Babylon was built. E Sagila was made perfect.
The gods, and the Anunaki together he made.
The holy city, the abode of the joy of their hearts, supremely he proclaimed.
Merodach a wide space on the face of the deep bound (it) round.
He made dust, and poured it on the space.
The gods in the abode of the joy of heart he seated.
He made mankind.
The goddess Aruru created the seed of humanity by him.
The cattle of the field, the living creatures of the field he made.
The Tigris and Euphrates he made, and in (their) places he placed.
Their names as good he declared.
Grass, marsh plants, reeds, and forest he made.
The verdure of the field he made.
The land, the pool, and the jungle?
Oxen, the young steer, the humped cow and her calf, the sheep of the fold.
The plantation, and the forest also.
The wild goat and the gazelle were protected by him.
The lord Merodach around the sea made an embankment.

This remarkable text bears on its face an indication of being a much more ancient document than those already considered in the early part of this chapter. It is incorporated into a magical library relating to the purification of the temple of Nebo at Borsippa; but a very little examination is necessary to see that it is not an original product of this school. The great prominence given to Merodach, who is represented as the creator of the world and the human race, as well as the frequent mention of the Absu, or Mystic ocean, and of Eridu, show that we have to deal with an adapted version of one of the oldest legends of the great priest-city of Eridu.

Such borrowing of legends and adapting them to local necessities was not uncommon, and there is one example which is most striking. The city of Assur, the capital of the Assyrian empire, was in reality a colonial city, long under the rule of viceroys dependent upon the court of Babylonia. When, however, Assyria became a great kingdom, the priests sought to attribute its foundation to the gods, and for this purpose compiled the following legend :—

"The god Assur opened his mouth, and said to the god Kir . . . above the deep (*Absu*), the abode of Ea before E Sarra, which I have built, below the two shrines I have made strong. When the god arose from the deep, thou didst prepare a place, unfinished it was, thou didst establish the city of Assur (*Pal-bi-ki*) with the temple of great gods. To his father Anu he spoke, even to him. The gods have appointed thee over whatsoever land thy hand has made, whatever thy hand possesses over the earth that thy hand has made, whatever thy hand possesses, the city of Assur of whom the name thou hast declared, the place which thou hast exalted for ever."

This legend, like the Creation one under consideration, is manifestly modelled on the literature of the schools of Eridu, especially the class of the magical tablets in which Merodach plays so important a part.

From this text it is evident that Merodach is regarded as the creator of all things, and he appears here in the same character as in the hymns, where he is invoked as the "Creator of mankind, even the black-headed race (Akkadians) and all living creatures that have received a name that exist in the world or the four quarters of the earth, wheresoever they are, all the angel host of heaven and earth, all (come from thee)." This is undoubtedly a hymn of the school of Eridu, and its contents are in exact agreement with the Creation text already translated.

The mention of the "reeds and marsh land" prove it to be a composition of a scribe of the Southern schools.

There is a very interesting relic of older times preserved in the last lines of the fragment, where we read, "The wild goat and the gazelle were protected by him." This carries us back to the days of totemism, and again serves to identify this legend with the oldest school of Chaldea. In Chaldea, as in Egypt, most of the gods had their sacred animals or totems in one form or another.

In the mythological inscriptions Merodach is called "the mighty one of the gazelle god," and as such the "gazelle" was his totem. So also as a solar deity "the goat" was one of his totems, and the goat-skin was the sacred robe of the Babylonian priests, as the panther skin was of the priests of Egypt.

The fact of this legend being, in its older form, a product of the school of Eridu is of great importance when we come to make such comparisons with the Biblical writings as are possible. Eridu, the Eridugga of the Akkadians, was the "Holy City," the abode of the god Ea and his son Merodach. Ea bore the titles of "the god who knows all things," "the lord of deep knowledge"—the Wise, and his abode was the *Absu,* or "House of deep knowledge" (*Bit nemiki*); it was, therefore, pre-eminently the city of Wisdom, and it is, therefore, most interesting to find a curious parallel, or series of similar thoughts and expressions, between this tablet and the "beginnings of wisdom," as described in the eighth chapter of Proverbs.

Portions, at least, of this remarkable Hebrew book are assigned to the ages of Solomon and Hezekiah, both periods of literary development among the Hebrew people, especially the latter, and it is interesting to find so striking a series of similarities.

| PROVERBS 8. 22-31. | INSCRIPTIONS. |
|---|---|
| The LORD possessed* me in the beginning† of his way, Before his works of old. I was‡ set up from everlasting. | The first-born ocean (Absu) was their generator. (*First tablet.*) |
| When there were no depths I was brought forth ; When there were no fountains abounding with water, Before the mountains were settled, Before the hills were brought forth, | The Absu (house of knowledge) was not made. In the midst of the sea was a flowing. |
| When as yet he had not made the earth or the fields, | The verdure of the field he made. |
| Nor the § highest part of the dust of the world. | He made the dust and poured it on the space. |
| When he prepared the heavens I was there ; When he set a circle upon the face of the depth, When he established the clouds above, When he ‖ strengthened the fountains of the deep, When he gave to the sea his decree, | Merodach made a wide space on the face of the deep, and bound it round. |
| That the waters should not pass his commandment, When he appointed the foundations of the earth, | The Lord Merodach around the sea made an embankment. |
| My delights are with the sons of men. | He made mankind, and the goddess Aruru made the seed of mankind by him. |

Here the resemblance is most striking when we regard Merodach as the representative of his father, the god of

---

* "Formed."    † "at the first."    ‡ "wrought."    § "heap of earth clods."
‖ "were fixed firmly."—Notes from *Variorum Bible*.

K

wisdom, and wisdom itself, the agreement is most remarkable.

There is much in the philosophical teaching of the school of Eridu, as shown in the hymns, litanies, and legends preserved in the British and other museums, which shows a curious resemblance to the conception of Wisdom in the Book of Proverbs, but these are outside of the present subject.

The flowing in the midst of the sea is evidently the *tide*, and this is supported by the reverse of the tablet, of which only a fragment remains; mention is also made of the goddess *Nin akha-kudda*, the daughter of Ea, who is called in other inscriptions the "lady of the rising waters of Ea." A comparison of this fragment with the first and second Tablets of the more complete series will show that it was in all probability from such documents that the compiler of this series derived his material.

## The Legend of Kutha.

This legend of Eridu is not the only one which have come to hand from the religious schools of Chaldea. There is a portion of one of the product of the school of Kutha, the sacred city of the god Nergal, the god of war and death. It is very mutilated, but it will be as well to quote it in order to complete our series of Creation Legends. In some respects this is a legend of evil creation rather than of good.

> (He is the lord) of all that is above, and that which is below, the
> lord of the spirits of earth;
> Who drinks turbid waters, and drinks not clear waters.
> He whose field is that where the warrior's weapon (*rests not*),
> he captures, he destroys.

EAGLE-HEADED FIGURE.
(Photographed from the original.)

On a tablet he wrote not, his mouth and bodies and produce he
  caused not to the land, and I drew not near him.
Warriors with the bodies of a bird of the valley, men with the
  faces of ravens did the great gods create.
In the earth the gods created his city.
Tiamat was their nurse;
Their progeny the mistress of the gods created.
In the midst of the mountains they grew up and became heroes,
  and increased in number;
Seven kings begotten appeared as fathers;
Six thousand in number were their hosts;
The god Banini was their father; their mother, the queen Niehili."

Here follow the names of the seven brothers. They are all in Akkadian and difficult of explanation, and may therefore be omitted. The various generations created seem to have been destroyed one after the other in much the same manner as Berosos describes the destruction of the composite creatures who preceded the organised creation.

The god then laments that all his efforts have only produced war and destruction, as each of these successive generations are destroyed. "Verily now, and I, what have I left to reign over? I am a king who brings not peace to his land, a prince who brings not peace to his hosts. Why have I established (only) corpses and left a desert? Terror of men: with night, death, and plague I have cursed it." This seems to indicate that it is a creation of evil by the dread god of war and death, and is evidently of so local a character as not to admit of any comparison with the Biblical account. The tablet is however interesting as enabling us to explain the eagle or raven-headed figures on the monuments, which seem to be beings belonging to a former creation, of a composite character, who had preceded the advent of man upon earth.

These inscriptions prove how in remote ages there had been drawn up various legends of the creation of the world, many of them presenting thoughts and conceptions of the work of the Creator similar to those found in the Hebrew writings. They, therefore, tend to shew how important the priests of Chaldea considered it, to possess among the religious documents of their schools of theology a carefully worded account of the beginnings of all things.

## CHAPTER III.

### THE SERPENT AND THE FALL.

THE serpent, or, more properly speaking, different kinds of serpents, held a considerable place in the religions of antiquity. The *rôle* of the serpent varies considerably in different systems; in some it appears as divine, protective, and benign. To this class belongs the Serpent of Ea—"the wise one," which is an emblem of life and wisdom. In other systems, on the contrary, it is the emblem of all that is evil and dark. In all religions we meet with the hostile night serpent and dragon—the wicked principle, which is the emblem of death and darkness. In the mythology of Babylonia this wicked Serpent is represented by the great dragon, Tiamat, which for myriads of years had coiled round the earth like a serpent around its egg, and whom, as I have already stated, is represented on the monuments as a serpent-limbed woman. The connection between the serpent and night, and, consequently, with the long first night which preceded the work of Creation, is proved by the monuments, for two great mystic serpents are mentioned in the inscriptions. The first is called *zir zalamtum*, "the Serpent of Darkness," or "the shadow of death"—the Hebrew *zalmoth*; the second is called the *zir musi*, or "Serpent of night." There is little trace of the war against the evil Serpent in the Hebrew writings; only a reference to it in the passage, "And Michael and his angels fought against the dragon ... and his angels" (Rev. 12. 7), and in the eternal enmity which was to exist between the seed of the mother Eve and the Serpent (Gen. 3. 15); yet both these passages are remarkably illustrated by the monuments. This is another evidence of the characteristic simplicity of the Hebrew account and its freedom from polytheistic elements which strangely enough keep touch with the thoughts of surrounding nations. All the poetic features of the great Nature war —one of the most universal of Nature myths—are found in the exploits of Ahuramazda, Indra Vishnu in the East, and of Apollo, Heracles, Kadmos, Odin, and Sigurd in the West. In the Hebrew record all this is summed up in two passages:—"And God said, let there be Light" (Gen. 1. 4), and "I will put enmity between thee and the woman, between thy seed and her seed; it shall bruise thy head, and thou shalt bruise his heel" (Gen. 3. 15). In the Babylonian record we have this same idea with a varied coating of polytheistic and mythic colouring.

The Nature war was an everlasting war, day by day and evening by evening it was commenced and ended. The Serpent slain, the Serpent again victorious, wounding the heel of the victor Merodach, the "protector of good men," the son of Ea, and the earth-mother, Davkina. In the myth, one of the chief opponents of Merodach, the son of Ea, is the great Serpent with seven heads and seven tails. This hydra-like conception was but the demon of the week, the hebdominal serpent. In the Babylonian mythology, Merodach was the Lord of Light, the opponent of Darkness. Light was synonymous with goodness, and so the Lord of Light became the "good one," as the Serpent of Darkness became the Evil One. In so poetic a school of religious thought as that of Babylonia, it can hardly be expected that so rich a theme as this would escape a copious

elaboration, and consequently the second, third, and fourth tablets of the Creation series are devoted to the Creation of Light, the War in Heaven, the defeat and curse of the Serpent, and, what is more important still, valuable traces of the Legend of the Fall. Tiamat is here treated as the Evil One, and is provided with a mysterious spouse, *Kingi*, whose name means the "maker of darkness." It is interesting to observe in the Babylonian legend the hostility is not only against the gods, but also against certain *divinely-created* beings who lived in a garden.

Is there any connection between this Serpent and the Temptation and the Fall? In several inscriptions the Serpent is called *aibu ilani*, "the enemy of the gods"; and that as early as the twelfth century before the Christian era it was regarded as a terrible power to inflict death and evil is shown by its mention in the imprecatory clauses on two boundary stones from Babylonia. On the Michaux Stone, in Paris, the writer says, "The emblems of the great gods and the *Serpent* on the written stone are recorded." On a fine memorial stone of Nebuchadnezzar I., king of Babylon, B.C. 1140, this Serpent-god is mentioned by name, and called *Shupu Ilu Shupu*, the Hebrew שְׁפִי *shipi*, "to glide";* while in another mythological tablet we find this Serpent mentioned as the ally of *Zir Khussu*, the "Hissing Serpents," who fight against the gods.

In the Hebrew account of the Fall, the Serpent is spoken of as "more subtil than any beast of the field" עָרוּם (*arūm*) (Gen. 3. 1). The inscriptions throw most highly important light upon this subject. The Serpent is, I have said, called the foe or enemy of the gods, *aibu*, the Hebrew

---

* See the important notes upon the use of this word by Delitzsch, *New Commentary on Genesis*, vol. i., p. 102.

איב (*oyeb*). In the tablets this word is equated with the Akkadian word *Erim*, and which means "to enchant," and the *Lu-Erim* was "the magician."

The word *Erim* bears so remarkable a resemblance to the Hebrew *arūm*, that it seems to be quite legitimate to regard it as borrowed. If this is the case, it throws much light on the *rôle* of the Serpent as a tempter. The Hebrew name of the Serpent, נָחָשׁ, *Nakhash*, is cognate with that of *Nakhson*, "divine" (Num. 1. 7), and both are cognate with the root נָחַשׁ, which has an undoubted magical signification, occurring in such phrases as, "observed times and enchantments" (2 Kings 21. 6), "neither shall ye use enchantments" (Lev. 19. 26), "to seek for enchantments" (Num. 28. 1). How appropriate this epithet was to the Serpent is shown by the Babylonian inscription:—

> Against the gods, my fathers, thy enmity thou hast directed.
> Thou enslaver of my companions,
> Stand up, I and thou will fight together.
> When Tiamat heard this
> She uttered her former spells, she repeated her words;
> Tiamat also cried vehemently with a high voice,
> She recited an incantation, she cast her spell.

Here, then, we have the direct association of the subtilty of the Serpent, and the witch or magician—a very remarkable comment on the curious phrase in the Bible (Gen. 3. 13), "the serpent beguiled me and I did eat." But this association was not only with magic, but also with death. The Serpent, who was the enemy of gods and men, was the offspring of the land of death, and is called *binut arali* or *binut bit muti*, "the creation of the house of death." The connection between death and the Serpent is common in most religions, but the association of the beguiler, enchanter,

ASSYRIAN TABLET OF THE CREATION SERIES.
(Photographed from the original.)

and death, is further borne out by the inscriptions, where the Lu-Erim, or magician, is called "the man in whose mouth is death," and the bite of the serpent is called "a touch of the mouth of death." The important point is, have we any trace of the story of the Fall in the Babylonian inscription? and, if so, is it in any way associated with death? The first indication is afforded by the seal figured in Mr. George Smith's Chaldean Genesis (p. 83), in which a scene in many ways resembling the Fall is represented. A man and woman are seated on either side of a tree, from whose branches hang rich bunches of fruit, and behind the woman a serpent is rearing up. The garden of the gods is represented upon several seals, notably one in the Hague Museum, and some in the Cesnola collection. In the Mythological Tablet, which is the third of the Creation series, is described the various wicked acts of the Serpent Tiamat:—

> The great gods, all of them determiners of fate,
> They entered, and, death-like, the god Sar filled.
> In sin one with the other in compact joins.
> The command was established in the garden of the god.
> The Asnan (fruit) they eat, they broke in two,
> Its stalk they destroyed:
> The sweet juice which injures the body.
> Great is their sin. Themselves they exalted.
> To Merodach, their redeemer, he appointed their fate.

It is almost impossible not to see in this fragment the pith of the story of the Fall, while the last line at once brings Merodach before us as the one who would defeat the Tempter and restore the fallen. The expression used is *mutir gimili su-nu*, "restorer of their benefit"—words all clearly Semitic.

L

KERUBIM.

In the ninth tablet of the Gilgames Legends this garden of the gods is described as "one with trees bearing crystal fruits and emerald leaves, and whose branches hang down with beautiful shade." Moreover, it is guarded by KERUBIM in the shape of scorpion men and women, who are thus described by the writer :—

> To the Mountains whose names is double,
> To the Twin Mountains, in his course he came,
> Which each day guard the Sun, rising
> Over them was the threshold of heaven,
> Below them the tomb sank down.
> Scorpion men who guard its gate;
> Burning with terribleness is their reverence—beholding them death.
> The greatness of their aspect sweeps the slopes of the hills;
> At the rising of the Sun and the setting of the Sun, they guard the Sun.

In this remarkable extract the most startling description of the Kerubim is given.

One other point remains to be noticed, and this is the crushing of the Tempter, which is described in the Babylonian Tablet in the following words :—

> Tiamat, whom he had bound, then turned backward.
> So Bel trampled on the belly of Tiamat:
> With his club unslung he smote her brain,
> He broke it, and caused her blood to flow;
> The North wind bore it away to secret places.

Here, then, is the victory of the seed of the woman. It is curious to notice the Babylonian Arali or House of Death, the abode of the Serpent, was placed in the north-east.

It may therefore be concluded that there are in the Babylonian records distinct traces of "the Story of the Serpent and the Fall in the Garden."

SEAL OF THE TEMPTATION.
(*Photographed from the original.*)

## CHAPTER IV.

### THE BEGINNING OF CIVILISATION.

THE Hebrew Scriptures, as well as most Oriental traditions, agree in placing the "beginning of civilisation" in that semi-mythic period before the Deluge. It was the age of the heroes; it was the age in which each caste of society sought to place its founder. The fourth chapter of Genesis has been aptly called by some writers the Hebrew Legend of Civilisation, for it is there the record is given of the first steps of the primitive forefathers on the pathway of civilisation. The chapter is a very remarkable one; as will be observed in the first place, it stands to a certain extent alone, being less connected with the narrative than others; and, in the second place, it is entirely, with the exception of the last two verses, the work of the Jehovist writer. This is an important point to consider when examined in its relation to monumental evidence. The structure of the Jehovist's narrative is very remarkable; it is he alone who records the Fall, and the beginning of Civilisation. According to him, any individual action on the part of man, such as the eating of the forbidden fruit, is an exaltation of himself in rivalry to God, and consequently a sin. So, also, his progress on the path of civilisation is assigned to the line of the cursed one, Cain the murderer is driven from the face of Jehovah. How curiously this is indicated even in the very first steps. The Fall is followed by the sense of nakedness and shame and the making of coats of fig-leaves, followed by the "making of coats of skins," which brings enmity between man and the brute creation (Gen. 3. 21).

In this fourth chapter there is, however, a very remarkable outline of the dawn of civilisation, and one which I venture to think has not received so much attention as it merits. There is a method and arrangement in the events, which indicates a careful study of the laws of racial development. From the first parents banished from Paradise are born two children—sons, Cain and Abel. These two become respectively the heads of the two earliest divisions of the human race—the agriculturist and the pastoral nomad. The two divisions established, there is an unceasing rivalry between them, as I have already pointed out when dealing with the Creation Legends. It exists to-day in the rivalry between the Bedawin and Fellahin as it did in the days of Mohammed, who said, "The Divine glory is among the shepherds, vanity and impudence among the agriculturists." This rivalry leads to a continual warfare. Indeed, among the agricultural Babylonians the word enemy was synonymous for a "nomad of the desert." This rivalry is shown in the struggle between the two brothers for the favour of the God of the land; and, according to the scheme of the Jehovist, "the tiller of the soil" is rejected and the "feeder of sheep" is accepted. The rivalry then leads to bloodshed, and the shepherd is slain by his agricultural brother. In the struggle for existence, the nomad goes down before the settler; the shepherd succumbs to the agriculturist. The first step of man on the path of civilisation is marked by hatred and bloodshed. The murderer is banished with the curse of Jehovah upon him. He leaves the land of Eden— "the field" or "plain"—and departs eastward to the land of Nod (Gen. 4. 16). This land, which has so long been unknown, is now identified by the aid of the monuments as the district to the east of the Tigris, one of the rivers of Eden, the land of the barbarians. It was inhabited by mixed races of hardy, warlike, plundering mountaineers—the Guti of the inscriptions, the Goïm of the Hebrews (Gen. 14, 1). In the rocky ranges of the districts of Kurdistan and Luristan had grown up kingdoms and tribal princedoms ever hostile to the Babylonians and the dwellers in Mesopotamia. The old kingdoms of Ansan, Elam, and later on Persia, were situated in this region. It was from this district that Cyrus marched to deliver the death blow to this "first of empires." In the inscriptions, mixed tribes of this district are called by the name of *Zab manda*, or "host of the manda." This word *manda* comes from the root *Nadu*, " to wander," and agrees with the expression of Cain, "I have become a fugitive and a wanderer " (Gen. 4, 14). Zabmanda became synonymous with "barbarian wanderer," and the land of Nod the "land of the barbarians," or "wanderers." It is probable that here is an echo of the origin of one element of Babylonian civilisation—that of the Akkadian "mountaineers" from the east of the Tigris.

**The First City.**—We now come to the next step in this remarkable chapter. Cain has a son, Enoch (Khanoch); " he builded a city, and called the name of the city after the name of the son, Enoch." Here we have a step in perfect accord with the laws of racial development. The agriculturist becomes a village dweller, from whom is born the town or city dweller.

Before considering this stage in the development of primitive man, it will be well to advance one stage further—" and unto Enoch was born Irad."

At this stage of study a little difficulty presents itself, as the two names admit of no clear etymological explanation by Hebrew; Enoch being explained as "dedicated," and Irad by "wild ass," neither of which statements are satisfactory in affording any solution.

If, however, we turn to Babylonian inscriptions, there is material that will assist us. It is universally admitted that Hebrew or Biblical names, which I prefer to call them, as they are not all Hebrew, have a meaning generally in some degree associated with the life or circumstances of the person or place indicated.

In Gen. 10. 10 one of the earliest of the cities of Nimrod, the city of Erech, is mentioned. This city was the first capital of the ancient Chaldean empire, and its name was *Uru-Ki*, "the city of the land"; but the Akkadian pronunciation of the ideograms of this name was *Unūg*, or *Unūk*, which, allowing for the strong gutteral pronunciation of the first character of either ע or ח, would make out a very slight corruption between it and *Khanoch*, or Enoch. It becomes, then, most clear that Khanoch, the name of the first city of Hebrew tradition, bears a close resemblance to *Unuk*, the first capital of Chaldea.

With regard to Irad, I should venture to suggest that this also is a Babylonian name, but slightly corrupted. In the south of Babylonia, on the shores of the Persian Gulf, was the great sacred city of Chaldea, a city which perhaps rivalled Uruk or Erech in antiquity. This town was called by the Akkadians *Eri-dugga*, "the holy city," which passed into Semitic Babylonian in the form *Eridu*, and is a very near approach to the Hebrew Irad. The suggestion receives very strong support from the Chaldean traditions as recorded by Berosos, which certainly make Eridu one

Ruins of the Palace of Gudea at Tello (*see page* 96).

of the cities where primitive civilisation in Babylonia first began. According to this Greco-Chaldean writer, we read: " In the first year there appeared in that part of the Erythean Sea (Persian Gulf) which borders on Babylonia a creature endowed with reason, by name Oannes, whose whole body was that of a fish; under the fish's head he had another head, with feet also below similar to those of a man subjoined to a fish's tail. His voice, too, and language were articulate and human, and a representation of him is preserved even to this day."

"This being was accustomed to pass the day among men, but took no food at that season; he gave them an insight into letters and sciences and arts of every kind. He taught them to construct houses, to found temples, to compile laws, and explained to them the principles of geometrical science. He made them to distinguish the seeds of the earth, and showed them how to collect the fruits; in short, he instructed them in everything which could tend to soften their manners and humanise their lives."\*

This mystical creature, Oannes, is certainly to be identified with Ea, " the god of the sea," the fish-god, and the god of wisdom of Chaldea, the seat of whose worship was in Eridu. I am, therefore, inclined to think that we have in both these names, Enoch and Irad, not so much personal names as those of cities.

**Beginnings of Music.**—The next stage is interesting, but a little difficult to explain. Lamech has two wives, Adah and Zillah. The former has two sons, " Jabal, the father of all such as dwell in tents and have cattle"

---

\* " Eusebios Chron.," Cory's translation.

(Gen. 4. 20), and Jubal was "the father of all such as hand the harp and organ," or [*pipe*] (4. 21). In the first it would seem as if it was a retrograde movement, but it is probably another tradition woven into the history. The second, however, is much more interesting, as it presents a record of the introduction of the arts of pleasure in the form of music. It appears at first strange that the arts of pleasure should be invented before those of utility, such as metal working, but this is not unusual; nearly all negro tribes, for example, have a system of music and musical instruments of some kind of which they are presumably fond, and this is the case in many tribes where the working of metals is unknown. The instruments described are the harp (*kinnor*), and the organ or pipe, *ugab*, upon which the Babylonian monuments fortunately throw very considerable light.

Among the ruins at Tello, the ancient Sirpurra, "the city of the bright light," in South Chaldea, M. de Sarzec discovered a very interesting monument, a sort of memorial of victory. The age of this monument is unknown, but it may with considerable certainty be placed as early as B.C. 3000. It represents a harper and a number of musicians playing pipes and cymbals.

In this sculpture we have a most striking illustration of the beginnings of music as recorded in this chapter (Gen. 4. 21). Unfortunately, the name of the harp in the inscriptions is unknown, but the flute player is often mentioned. The flute was called *Gi-bu*, " the long reed," and flutes were used in the services of the temples.

**Metal Working.**—The invention of the arts of utility is attributed to the hero Tubal-Cain. In our A.V. we

Harper and Choir, b.c. 3000.

read, "an instructor of every artificer in brass and iron" (Gen. 4. 22), but which may be more clearly read "a forger of every instrument in copper and iron."* The working of the metals naturally implies the use of fire, and of the knowledge of the art of kindling fire. We therefore find in most ancient religous systems that the working of the metals is associated with the fire god.

The explorations of M. de Sarzec at Tello on the Shat-el Hie, in Southern Babylonia, brought to light the ruins of a very ancient city. This city Sirpurra, "the bright light or flame," as its name indicates, was dedicated to the god Ningirsu. Most of the inscriptions are those of a monarch named Gudea (*Prophet*), whose reign was about B.C. 2800; but there are many monuments of a far greater antiquity, reaching back to about B.C. 4000. The most archaic of these have inscriptions in a curious linear character, almost pictorial, which preceded the elaboration of the cuneiform writing. All the monuments contain dedications to "Ningirsu, the warrior of Ellila" ("the lord of the ghost land"). This god was the fire god of Babylonia, and his worship was closely associated with the working of the metals.

The inscriptions and monuments from Tello enable us to ascertain the nature and character of this god. The name Ningirsu means simply "the piercer of the flesh," or mass; one form of his worship was of a character prevalent in all Oriental religions, but which cannot be discussed here. The city is sacred to the fire-god, and from the inscriptions we learn that its temple was called "the house of the fire-brand," or "fire wood." In many of the inscriptions

---

* See *Variorum Bible.*

from Tello the god Ningirsu is associated with "the lord of the wood of life." Taking all these points together, there is no difficulty in identifying, as I did many years ago, Ningirsu with "the fire god," and the "god of the fire stick." He was, in fact, the Prometheus of Chaldea, and therefore Sirpurra, becomes the Pyropolis, or Fire City, of Chaldea. I would here make a suggestion—it is but a suggestion—that Ningirsu was the upper or revolving fire stick; the piercer of the flesh, or robber; the Arani of the Vedas, who draws the hidden fire from the Gis-zida, or "wood of life," the lower stick in which the fire was hidden. A fire drill complete was found by Prof. Flinders Petrie at Kahun, in the Fayoum, in Egypt.

The figures in the illustration afford ample proof of this. The attitude of the god holding in his hand the cone is exactly that assumed by a person using the fire stick. Beside this, is a figure of the fire god found at Khorsabad, the palace of Sargon II. (B.C. 722).

The association of the fire god with the City of Gudea is thus of great importance from an archæological point of view. To explain this, I will quote a hymn to the fire god from a tablet in the British Museum :—

> The fire god, the prince who is mighty in the land;
> The warrior, the son of the deep, who is high in the land.
> Oh, Fire God! by thy pure fire
> In the house of darkness thou makest light.
> Thou determinest the destiny of all that is called by name
> Of bronze and lead; thou art the mingler.
> Of silver and gold thou art the purifier;
> Thou art he that turnest away the breast of the evil man at night.

This hymn, it will be seen, associates the fire god with the working of metals, and it is therefore not surprising to

BRONZE FIGURES, B.C. 2800.
(*Photographed from the original.*)

FIRE-GOD, B.C. 722.

find some fine specimens of metal work in the excavations at Tello. These examples show the skill which the Babylonians had attained to at so early an age. The knowledge of bronze casting must have been acquired very early, as we find it referred to in the hymns, where the man purified of sin is said to shine like " bronze poured out of the crucible." The work of the age of Gudea shows considerable advance on primitive work, for it is chased, and has been inlayed with gold in the decorations of the dress, as shown by two statues of Ningirsu in the British Museum. Some little figures were found which belong to an age very much more remote, and were discovered in the lowest strata of the ruins with monuments of so archaic a character as to necessitate them being placed at a period as far back as at least B.C. 4000. With these discoveries I shall deal later on. This early metal working is most interesting, as it throws so much light upon the Hebrew record of early civilisation contained in Gen. 4, where the working of bronze and iron is attributed to Tubal Cain (*ib.* 4. 22). Iron is not mentioned in these inscriptions. There is, however, a very valuable passage relating to the metals in an inscription upon a large statue; the king, speaking of his statue, says, "Neither in silver or in copper or in tin or in bronze let anyone undertake the execution." The separate mention of tin and copper followed by bronze indicates a knowledge of making an amalgam of these metals. Gold is only mentioned as gold dust.

Much uncertainty exists with regard to the original working of iron, as, owing to its rapid oxidisation, deposits of iron tools become soon destroyed. Dr. Flinders Petrie*

---

\* "Ten Years' Digging," p. 152.

places it as late as B.C. 800. Iron may have been known as a curiosity, just as one example of bronze occurs two thousand years before it came into actual use; but it had no effect on the arts. A discovery made by Mr. W. Bliss in the excavations at Tel Hesy, the site of the ancient Amorite fortress of Lacish, in Southern Palestine, carries it back later. He discovered the remains of a large smelting furnace, with a considerable deposit of slag at the bottom. The slag has been analysed by Dr. Adams, Professor of Chemistry at Beyrout, and pronounced to be iron and silicon, with no trace of copper. This furnace was on a layer, which, from other objects around, cannot be assigned to a later date than B.C. 1400. Upon the scarcity of iron, not necessarily indicating a want of knowledge of this metal and the modes of obtaining it, I may quote the words of Prof. Remsen, of Baltimore, who says, "The suggestion has been made that it is less difficult to extract iron from its ores than to make bronze; possibly iron was used as early as bronze, but owing to the fact that iron easily rusts, implements of this metal have disappeared, while those of bronze remain." It is, therefore, within all the bounds of possibility that the Hebrew writer is correct in assigning an early age to iron working.

Thus, then, it will be seen that not only in every step, but in almost every detail of those individual steps, the growth of culture in Babylonia corresponds with the outline given in this remarkable chapter in Genesis.

**Cain and Abel.**—A curious echo of the Legend of Civilisation is found in one of the tablet books of the Epic of Chaldea, the Story of Gilgames, or Nimrod, and it presents a strange resemblance to the Hebrew story in the arrangement of the episodes. In the sixth tablet of the series, Istar, the goddess, has fallen in love with Gilgames, or Nimrod, the king of the city of *Unug* (Enoch), or Erech. The tablet begins with a proposal of marriage from the goddess,—

> For the favour of Gilgames Istar, the princess, lifted her eyes.
> Look, Gilgames, and be thou my bridegroom;
> Be thou my husband, and I will be thy wife, etc.

After a long address, the hero taunts her with the harm she has done her former lovers. "Never," he says, "may I be thy bridegroom for ever, never may any god make thee happy. Go, I will tell thee the story of thy enslavements." Among the lovers are two whose stories afford a curious resemblance to those of Cain and Abel, and are probably old-folk legends of the myth of civilisation.

"Thou didst love the shepherd Tabulu, who continually poured out for thee the smoke of sacrifices. Every day he was slaughtering victims for thee; thou didst drive him forth, and into a jackal didst change him. His own sheep cote drove him away, and his own dogs tore his flesh." In this story, so closely resembling the myth of Actæon, we have the shepherd sacrificing to the mother goddess. In the next story: "Moreover, thou didst love Isullanu, the gardener of thy father (*Anu*), who was for ever raising for thee costly trees. Every day he made bright thy plate. Thou didst take from him his sight, and didst mock him." The names are interesting, Tabulu being a derivation from the same root as Abel, while Isullanu is explained by "he who makes living things green."

Having thus established the existence in Babylonia of legends of civilisation closely similar, it may not be out of place to examine some of the features of this primitive culture.

**Akkadian Civilisation.**—The discoveries of recent years have given an immense retrospective enlargement to our knowledge of Oriental history, and especially that of Chaldea. Inscriptions have been deciphered so archaic in character as to seem almost mere scratchings, and revealed languages most primitive in construction, but still the products of centuries of thought and labour. Artistic remains have been discovered in the ruins of Chaldean cities dating back thirty and forty centuries before the Christian Era, which show that there, as in Egypt, the beginnings of art are lost in the remote past. To begin with the linguistic affinities. The language of the cuneiform inscriptions on the statues and bricks from these cities is an agglutinative one, allied to the language of the early Elamite population and the proto-Median dialect of the people of Ansan, its modern affinities being found in the Ugro Finnic and Tartar dialect; while, as Drs. Terrien de Lacouperie and Ball have shown, there is a distinct linguistic relationship between these primitive tongues and the language of Early China—that introduced by the Bak tribes, the so-called Hundred Families. Linguistically their position is not difficult to define as belonging to the Turanian family and the Tartar branch of that group, with a close affinity to the languages of Central Asia—a district through which they passed at an early period.

**Racial Types.**—We will now examine such racial types as the monuments afford, and endeavour to see to what extent they agree with the evidence of language.

The type of the first face in the illustration would be at once assigned to the Turanian branch, and resembles exactly the features of the Elamites of the monuments and the Tartars of Central Asia. Above all we have the turban, a most characteristic feature. The second head is more difficult to class, owing to its being shaved. It is manifestly that of a *gallu* or priest, and should, I think, be classed also as belonging to the same family; it is certainly not Semitic. In the older monuments, such as the *Stele of the Vultures*, we get as far as the archaic work will admit an identification,—a Turanian and very Chinese or Mongol type, with even faint traces of the pig tail.

There is, therefore, an undoubted agreement between the ethnographical and linguistic evidence in classing this primitive population of Chaldea as belonging to the Tartar and Mongol branch of the great Turanian family.

**Social Life.**—The social details of the life of the community as described in the inscriptions indicate a primitive organisation to which the monuments have not before afforded us access. The Babylonian and Assyrian religious texts had made us familiar with the fact that the creed of Turanian primitive Chaldea was a religio-magic similar to that of the Shamans of Tartary, but no historical or contemporary evidence of the actual existence of such a creed was forthcoming. The inscriptions of Tello show, however, that this weird religion still held its position in the days of Gudea; although the spirits had become gods, and the temple replaced the tent of the medicine man. When Gudea ascended the throne he says, "Then the city he made pure; he cleansed it, when he laid the foundation of the temple and deposited the record. The callers of demons, the seers of spirits, the charmers, the wives of muttering (witches), from the city he drove out; who ever went not willingly by the soldiers was expelled." This shows us clearly the primitive age we have to deal with. The solemn act of the king must be interfered with by no muttered charm or magician's spell; no evil eye must be cast upon the work. The king then describes the great period of peace which he had chosen for the work of building the temple. No malevolent influences existed, no death had taken place, "no female mourner had caused her lamentation to be heard," the plaintiff to place of the oath had not gone, "no robber to the house of a man had entered." It was a time of peace, "a fortunate day at the commencement of the year." A calendar which I published some years ago showed how this superstition as to lucky and unlucky days affected every detail of primitive Babylonian life, and no doubt Gudea had examined every sign and omen before undertaking his pious work. We have now the record of a most curious custom, a species of public holiday. "Penalties I have remitted, gifts I have given." For seven days service was not exacted. The female slave has been made the equal of her mistress, the male slave the equal of his master. The chief to his vassal has been made the equal. This curious week of communal life is of great interest, as it must be the survival of a very primitive age indeed. It is, however, manifestly the same as the festival of the Sakœa mentioned by Berosos, "when for five days the masters should obey their servants." It is to be noted here that the female slave is mentioned along with her mistress, and before the male slave and his master.

**Position of Women.**—One of the most interesting and characteristic features of this civilisation was the high position of women. The mother here is always represented by a sign which means "the goddess of the house." Any sin against the mother, any repudiation of the mother, was punished by banishment from the community. These facts are evidently indicative of a people who had at one time had the law of matriarcal descent. In the hymns we find in the Sumirian version "female and male" the order; while in the Semitic texts it is "male and female." Another example of this equality of women of a most interesting character is afforded by this passage. Speaking of the offerings to his statue the king says, "The house were there is no son the *daughter* with new (?) offerings has entered; before the face of the statue she has placed them." This freedom once accorded to women in the primitive times was never withdrawn entirely, and thus in the later Babylonian times we find women exercising almost equal rights with the men. This high position of woman in the community is another very distinct mark of the Turanian character of this early people, and has been noticed as still surviving among the tribes of Central Asia by Professor Vambery.*

**Peaceful Character.**—The whole characteristic of this early community is one of peace and plodding self improvements, with no aggressive elements. Only one war is recorded, and that is against the national foe, the land of Ansan, afterwards the Elamite kingdom. From

---

\* It may be this high estimate of women that led to the mention of Adah, Zillah, and Naamah in the Hebrew beginning of civilisation.

the earliest times, earlier even than the days of Gudea, the Elamite was the born foe of the people of Chaldea, and between them there was a never-ceasing border feud. How truly an hereditary antipathy this was may be seen when the old Nature war becomes the national epic. Khumbaba, the old storm-god, the everlasting enemy of the solar hero, is transformed into Khumbaba the Elamite. The one war of Gudea is described as "By arms the city of Ansan in the land of Elam he has conquered; its spoils to the god Ningirsu he has consecrated."

**Sacred Statues.**—The statues of Gudea had a curious religious position. They were placed in the temple as everlasting representations of the king always to be before the god and remembered by him. Certain offerings were instituted " of food, beer, oil and meal," and under a severe penalty these were not to be revoked. On one of the statues we read, " Gudea unto the statue has given a command, to the statue of my king speak thou." The figure was really an embodiment of the king in the temple for ever; it was, like the Egyptian *Ka* statue, inhabited by the spirit of the king, and fed by the *Ka* offerings made to it. The statue was a most sacred object, to be protected by all the laws of ancestor worship, for thus the king speaks regarding it: "Who ever shall transgress my judgments, revoke my gifts, or in the recitation of my prayers shall suppress my name and insert his own"—then shall he be cursed with a bitter curse :—

> Like an ox shall he be slain in the midst of his prosperity!
> Like a wild bull shall he be felled in the fullness of his strength!
> As for his throne, may those even whom he has bound captive overthrow it in the dust.

Statue of Gudea, b.c. 2800.

His name in the temple of his god may they erase from the tablets.
May his god upon the ruin of his country not look!
May he ravage it with the rains from heaven!
May he ravage it with waters of the earth!
May he become a man without a name!
May his princely race be reduced to slavery.
May this man as every man who acted evilly to his chief from under the vault of heaven, in no city find a resting place.

Such was the great excommunication pronounced against any who injured the royal statue. It is interesting to find this curse already formulated as early as 2800 B.C., for in it is the same as the curse which appears on all the Kudurri or boundary stones until quite later—for in Chaldee cursed indeed was he who removed his neighbour's land-mark.

I have now described the principal features of the art and civilisation of the age of Gudea; its high standard is beyond doubt, and far distant as it is, nearly forty-eight centuries ago, its progress indicates long centuries of previous development. Generations of toiling, plodding human beings, each adding its quota to build up this stage of the great learning and wisdom of Chaldea.

The civilisation of Ancient Chaldea presents many very remarkable characteristics. Its chief feature, however, is its evident self-development. The ancient Akkadeans were a contented home-dwelling people, with little desire to exhibit an aggressive policy either in trade or war, and consequently we find the basis of many of the laws of social life laid down by them. Among these simple laws we notice those of the family especially, which, even in the days of the powerful Semitic dynasties, were never eradicated. One of the most beautiful features of these early laws is the high position accorded to women. The control of the family by the mother, who is called the goddess of the house, the power of women to hold property, to make their own wills, and to act as parties to, or witnesses of contracts, were never lost. So also the laws of master and servant, the relations of landlord and tenant were set forth on a simple primitive basis which was a lasting one, and which formed the rule upon which many surrounding lands based their laws. In fact, we can see in this remarkable civilisation, the result of plodding and practical experience, many of the simple laws which constitute to this day the groundwork of Sociology.

## CHAPTER V.

### THE DELUGE.

THERE are preserved among Oriental traditions of the great Deluge, three which stand out as pre-eminently ancient:—The Hebrew records in Genesis (chaps. 6—9); the versions of the Chaldean tradition, preserved in the writings of the Greco-Chaldean historian Berosos; and to these we may now add the more ancient version of the original Chaldean inscription from which Berosos at least derived his account. The story of the discovery of the Chaldean inscriptions—which took place about twenty years ago, by the late Mr. George Smith—is well known, but it requires recapitulation, in order that at the outset of the study the position that this legend holds in the mass of Chaldean literature may be clearly understood.

The very direct references in the Scriptures (Gen. 10. 8–10; Mic. 5. 6) to Nimrod as the great hero of Chaldea, as well as the numerous legends of Hebrew, Arab, and Greek writers, always led the decipherers to hope that some day there would be revealed, from beneath the dust of centuries, the legends which the Chaldeans themselves had of this Eponym of their nation. In 1872 Mr. Smith found a number of a series of tablets which related to a hero, who was "a mighty-one on Earth," bearing the title of "the Warrior, perfect in strength," who distinguished himself in war and in the hunting field.

It was evident from the descriptions of this hero's great deeds that he was the same person as that powerful giant god so often represented in the Assyrian sculptures at Khorsabad and on the engraved Cylinder Seals. Other fragments of these tablets having been obtained from the East, it was found that the series of tablets when complete consisted of twelve tablet-books, each one corresponding to one of the twelve deeds or labours of this Chaldean Hercules. The hero of this cycle of poems is called Gilgames, a name which is of non-Semitic — probably Akkadian—origin, and means the "mass of fire"; and the series of tablet-books are known by the name of Zikar Gilgames, "the story of Gilgames."

The epithets applied to him are nearly all solar, as in a hymn addressed to the solar hero he is called "Gilgames, the King perfect in Strength, the Judge of the Spirits, the Exalted Prince, the Chief of Mankind, the Watchman of the Four Quarters, the Glory of the Earth, the Lord of the Underworld." All these epithets are applied to the Sun god in other hymns, so that, guided by these facts, and by the character of the legends preserved, Sir Henry Rawlinson was able to point out the solar character of the Epic of Chaldea.

We find that the Eleventh Tablet, which, according to this arrangement, should correspond to the "month of the curse of rain," and to the sign of Aquarius, has woven into its columns the story of the Deluge.* It is therefore clear that the tale of the preservation of the Chaldean Sage— whose name in the tablet is Samas-Napisti, "the Sun of Life," or "the Living Sun," the Xisuthrus of Berosos, the

---

* There are indications of several legends older than the Epic being woven in when it was given literary form.

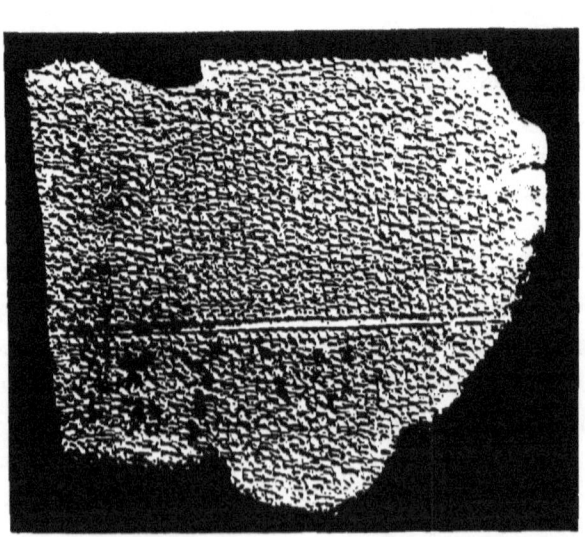

Deluge Tablet (Portion of the Eleventh Tablet of the Chaldean Epic).
(Photographed from the original.)

Noah of the Hebrew record—is here boldly interpolated into the Epic as an episode, to keep it in harmony with the Zodiacal arrangement. This is shown by the fact that at line 8, in column i., it is ruled off from the rest of the story. We have been able to recover by the decipherment of this series of legends the originals of many of the traditions of Nimrod, and also a far older legend embodied in the Epic,—the story of the Deluge.

The preceding tablet, the tenth, specifies that the hero, sick and afflicted, covered with leprosy and deprived of his hair, wherein, like the Hebrew Samson, lay his strength, is journeying to learn the secret of immortality. This secret—"the hidden thing of the gods" as it is here called—can only be revealed by the ancient Sage Samas-Napisti, who has been translated by the gods to dwell as one of themselves in immortality on an island near the mouths of the Tigris and Euphrates. To this remote island he is guided by the Chaldean Charon, a mythic personage named Nis-Ea, "the man of Ea," that is, the servant of the Water god—of whom I have already spoken in the chapter on the Creation Tablets—who pilots him across the river and waters of Death to this land where the translated sage lives. Having reached the place, the hero speaks to the Chaldean Noah, and lays before him the object of his visit. "Gilgames to him, even Samas-Napisti the remote, spake: I am burdened with a decree. The cure thou repeatest not to me, even thou—the rest of thy heart from making tribulation . . . . to thee I am come up. What hast thou laid hold of, (that) in the assembly of the gods thou art placed?" The translated sage then proceeds "to relate the story of his preservation"; the next 173 lines are occupied with an account of the Deluge and the translation of Samas-

Napisti. There are many indications that this story is much older than the complete Epic of Gilgames; and even in the tablets the commencement of the story is carefully lined off from the rest of the inscription.

Before passing to the comparative analysis of this inscription, it may be well to refer to one or two facts bearing on this historical character which the Chaldeans have attached to the Deluge. One of the strongest pieces of evidence is to be found in the Tablet of Royal Names (W. A. I., vol. v., pl. 47), where the important gloss appears: " These are kings ruling after the Deluge (*Abubi*), who according to their relative order wrote not." In like manner the story of the preservation of Sargon, of Agadhe or Akkad, in an ark of bulrushes on the Euphrates, and his elevation to the throne, may be a transference of the Deluge tradition to this hero of the Semites, whose remote antiquity (3750 B.C.) might cause him to become tinged with a mythic glamour. The Deluge formed the rubicon between the mythic period and the heroic and polyarchal age, separating the reigns of local kings from the far distant age of the ten antediluvian Patriarchs.

The genealogy of the hero of the Deluge is given in the tablet (col. i. 20) : " Oh, Man of the City of Surippak, Son of Ubarratuti." This latter is the Obartes or Ortiartes of Berosos, who was king of Larancha, according to the Greek text, but which M. Lenormant has shown was a corruption of Surippak ("La Langue Primitive," p. 342). The name Xisuthrus, which Berosos gives to the Chaldean Noah, may be a corruption of the epithets Adra Khasis, "reverent and holy," applied to the hero in col. i. 45, and in col. iv. 22; but it is hardly possible—the more likely solution being that it is a Hellenicised form of Zi-Susru, "the Spirit of the Founder," and perhaps such an etymology may explain the translation of Xisuthrus, recorded by Berosos: "They remaining within (the ark), finding their companions did not return, quitted the vessel with many lamentations, calling continually on the name of Xisuthrus. Him they saw no more; but they could distinguish his voice in the air, and hear him admonish them to pay due regard to religion." The City of Surippak, of which Samas-Napisti or Xisuthrus was king, is called "the Ship City" (W. A. I., ii. 46, 1), and the Lord of the city was the god Ea—the god of rivers, seas, and ships—who takes so prominent a part in this legend in protecting the sage. He is here called "the Lord of Ships—Ea, the Lord of Surippak" (W. A. I., ii. 60, 21). The name of the father of Samas-Napisti, Ubarra-Tutu, is explained in the syllabaries and bilingual tablets as Ubarra = Kidinu—"Servant" (W. A. I., ii. pl. 3, No. 254); and the god Tutu is given in the bilingual list of Royal Names as the synonym of Marduk or Merodach (W. A. I., v. 42, 18). In a bilingual tablet (K. 2107), the god Tutu is called *Muallad ili Muddis ili* —"the generator and restorer of the gods"—in which character he may be identified with Merodach as the god of the dawn and twilight. In this relationship Samas-Napisti, "the Living Sun," would be the child of the "Servant of the Dawns," as this name means— rising each day at his message, and setting each day by his decree.

| Chaldean Deluge Tablet. | Hebrew Narrative. | |
|---|---|---|
| | Jehovistic Account. | Elohistic Account. |
| Column I. | | |
| *Story Commences.* | | |
| Line | | |
| 9 Let me reveal to thee, Oh! Gizdhubar, the story of my preservation | | |
| 10 And the hidden thing of the Gods let me tell to thee | | |
| 11 The City of Surippak, which thou knowest is placed on the Euphrates | | |
| 12 That City was very ancient (when) the Gods within it | | |
| *Decision of the Gods.* | | |
| 13 To make a Deluge the great Gods brought their Hearts | And Yahveh saw that the wickedness of man was great in the earth, and that every imagination of the thoughts of his heart was only evil continually. And it repented Yahveh that he had made man on the earth, and it grieved him at his heart. And Yahveh said, I will destroy man whom I have created from the face of the ground; both man and beast, and creeping thing, and | And the earth was corrupt before Elohim, and the earth was filled with violence. And Elohim saw the earth, and, behold, it was corrupt; for all flesh had corrupted his way upon the earth. And Elohim said unto Noah, The end of all flesh is before me; for the earth is filled with violence through them; and behold, I will destroy them with the earth. |
| 14 Their Father Anu their King; their | | |
| 15 Counsellor the Warrior Bel; their | | |
| 16 Throne-bearer the God Adar, and | | |
| 17 The God Ea, the Lord of the underworld | | |
| 18 Repeated their decree | | |
| 19 I this destiny hearing (as) he said to me | | |
| 20 Oh! Man of Surippak, son of Ubaratutu | | |
| 21 Destroy the House and build a Ship | | |
| 22 For I will destroy the Seed and the Life | | |
| 23 Cause them to go up into the Ship all seed that hath Life | | |

## BUILDING OF THE ARK.

| Chaldean Deluge Tablet—*cont.* | Hebrew Narrative—*cont.* | |
|---|---|---|
| | JEHOVISTIC ACCOUNT. | ELOHISTIC ACCOUNT. |
| | fowl of the air; for it repenteth me that I have made them. But Noah found grace in the eyes of Yahveh.<br><br>And Yahveh said unto Noah, Come thou and all thy house into the ark; for thee have I seen righteous before me in this generation. Of every clean beast thou shalt take to thee seven and seven the male and his female: of the fowl also of the air which are clean, seven and seven, male and female; and of birds which are not clean two, male and female; to keep seed alive upon the face of all the earth. | |
| *Form of the Ark.*<br>line<br>24, 25 The Ship which thou shalt make — cubits its length in measure<br>26 — cubits the contents of its breadth and height<br>27 — above the deep roof it over<br>28 I understood, and said to Ea, my Lord | | Make thee an ark of cypress wood; cells shalt thou make in the ark; . . . And this is how thou shalt make it; the length of the ark three hundred cubits, the breadth of it fifty cubits, and the height of it thirty cubits. A light shalt thou make to the ark, |

## Chaldean Deluge Tablet—*cont.*

Line
29 The building of the Ship which thou commandedst
30 If it be made by me
31 Then will laugh at me, the children of the people, and the old men

### Warning of the Deluge.

32 Ea opened his mouth and spake to me, his servant
33 If they laugh at thee, thou shalt say to them
34 Every one who has turned from me
35 Shall be punished, for the protection of the Gods is over me
36
37 I will judge my judgment upon all above and below
38 Close not the Ship
39 Until the season, when I shall send thee word (saying)
40 "Enter the Ship and close the door"

### Provisioning the Ark.

41 In the interior of it, thy grain, thy furniture, thy goods
42 Thy wealth, thy man-servants and maid-servants and thy young men

## Hebrew Narrative—*cont.*

### JEHOVISTIC ACCOUNT.

### ELOHISTIC ACCOUNT.

and to a cubit shalt thou finish it upward; and the door of the ark shalt thou set in the side thereof; with lower, second, and third stories shalt thou make it.

And I, behold, I do bring the deluge of water upon the earth, and destroy all flesh, wherein is the breath of life, from under heaven; every thing that is in the earth shall die. But I will establish my covenant with thee;

And of every living thing of all flesh, two of every sort shalt thou bring into the ark, to keep them alive with thee; they shall be

DELUGE TABLET, No. 2.
A number of pieces making oblong tablet.
(Photographed from the original.)

# Trying the Ark.

| Chaldean Deluge Tablet—*cont.* | Hebrew Narrative—*cont.* | |
|---|---|---|
| | Jehovistic Account. | Elohistic Account. |
| Line | | |
| 43 The cattle of the field and the animals of the field as many as I would preserve | | male and female. Of the fowl after their kind, and of the cattle after their kind, and of every creeping thing of the ground after its kind, two of every sort shall come unto thee to keep them alive; and take thou of all food that is eaten, and gather it to thee; and it shall be food for thee and for them. |
| 44 I will send to thee (then) make firm thy door | | |
| 45 The Reverent and Holy One opened his mouth and spake to Ea, his Lord | | |
| 46 No one has made such a Ship | | |
| 47     on the ground (to hold all things) | | |
| 48 [The form of] the Ship let me see | | |
| *Proving the Ark.* | | |
| 49 And on the ground I will make the Ship which thou commandest | | |
| Column II. | | |
| | And Noah did according unto all that Yahveh commanded him. | Thus did Noah; according to all that Elohim commanded him, so did he. |
| 2 On the fifth day two sides were raised | | |
| 3 In its enclosure (hull) fourteen ribs | | |
| 4 Also fourteen they numbered above | | |
| 5 I placed its roof and enclosed it | | |
| 6 Sixthly I made it firm, seventhly I divided its passages | | |
| *Pitching the Ark.* | | |
| 7 Eighthly its interior I examined | | And shalt pitch it within and without with pitch. |
| 8 Openings to the Waters I stopped | | |

## Chaldean Deluge Tablet—cont.

Line
9 I searched for cracks and the wanting parts I fixed
10 Three sari of bitumen I poured over the Outside
11 Three sari of bitumen I poured over the Interior
12 Three sari of men bearers who carried chests on their heads
13 I kept a saros of chests for my people to eat
14 Two sari of chests I divided among the Boatmen
15 To the Gods I caused Oxen to be sacrificed
16 I appointed the portions for each day
17 and Wine
18 I gathered like the Waters of the river
19 And food as the dust of the Earth
20 In receptacles my hand placed
21 With the help of the Sun God, the Ship was completed
22 All was made strong and—
23 And above and below the tackling was fixed
24 Then of my possessions I took two-thirds
25 All I had of Silver I gathered together
26 All I had of Gold I gathered together
27 All I had of the Seed of Life I gathered together the whole

## Hebrew Narrative—cont.

## COMMENCEMENT OF THE DELUGE.

| Chaldean Deluge Tablet—*cont.* | Hebrew Narrative—*cont.* | |
|---|---|---|
| | Jehovistic Account. | Elohistic Account. |
| *Entering the Ark.*<br>Line<br>28 I caused them all to be carried up into the Ship. All my Men-servants and Maid-servants.<br>29 The cattle of the field and the Beast of the field and the Young Men, all of them, I caused to go up<br><br>*Final Warning.*<br>30 The season the Sun God had fixed, and (of which) he spake, saying;<br>31 "I will cause it to rain from Heaven heavily,"<br>32 "Enter into the midst of the Ship and close thy door"<br>33 (That) season fixed came round (of which)<br>34 He spake saying; "I will cause it to rain from Heaven heavily" | And Noah went in, and his sons and his wife and his son's wives with him, into the ark, because of the waters of the deluge Of clean beasts, and of beasts that are not clean, and of clean fowls and of fowls that are not clean, and of every thing that creepeth upon the ground, there went in two and two unto Noah into the ark, male and female, as [Yahveh] had commanded Noah.<br><br>For yet seven days, and I will cause it to rain upon the earth forty days and forty nights: and every living thing that I have made will I destroy from off the face of the ground. | In the selfsame day entered Noah, and Shem and Ham and Japheth, the sons of Noah, and Noah's wife and the three wives of his sons with him, into the ark; they, and every beast after its kind, and all the cattle after their kind, and every creeping thing that creepeth upon the earth, after its kind, and every fowl after its kind, every bird of every sort; and they went in unto Noah into the ark, two and two of all flesh wherein is the breath of life. And they that went in went in male and female of all flesh, as Elohim commanded him |

| Chaldean Deluge Tablet—*cont.* | Hebrew Narrative—*cont.* | |
|---|---|---|
| | Jehovistic Account. | Elohistic Account. |
| *Closing the Ark.* | | |
| Line | | |
| 35 Of that day when I reached the twilight | And Yahveh shut him in. | |
| 36 The day which I had watched for with fear | | |
| 37 I entered into my Ship and closed my door | | |
| 38 That I might close my Ship to Buzur Sadairabu | | |
| 39 The Boatman, the great House, I gave with all its goods | | |
| *The Deluge.* | | |
| 40 Then rose the Water of dawn at daylight | And it came to pass after the seven days that the waters of the deluge were upon the earth. | And the waters prevailed, and increased greatly upon the earth; and the ark went upon the face of the waters; And the waters prevailed exceedingly upon the earth; and all the high mountains that were under the whole heaven were covered. Fifteen cubits upwards did the waters prevail; and the mountains were covered. |
| 41 Like a black cloud on the horizon of Heaven | | |
| 42 The thunder God in the midst of it thundered | | |
| 43 Nebo and the Wind God march in front | | |
| 44 The throne bearers (Storm Clouds) go o'er the mountain and plain | | |
| 45 The Pestilence God brings with him Affliction | | |
| 46 The War God goes in front and casts down | | |
| 47 The Angels of Earth carry the destruction | | |
| 48 In their glory they swept through the Land | | |
| 49 The Deluge of the Rain God reaches to Heaven | | |
| 50 The darkened Earth to waste is turned | | |

| Chaldean Deluge Tablet—*cont.* | Hebrew Narrative—*cont.* | |
| --- | --- | --- |
| | Jehovistic Account. | Elohistic Account. |
| Column III. | | |
| Line | | And all flesh died that moved upon the earth, both fowl and cattle, and beast and every creeping thing that creepeth upon the earth, and every man ; |
| 1 The surface of the Earth like fire they sweep | | |
| 2 They destroyed all Life from the face of the Earth | | |
| 3 To battle against Men they brought the Deluge | | All in whose nostrils was the breath of the spirit of life, of all that was in the dry land, died. |
| 4 Brother saw not Brother, Men knew one another | | And the waters prevailed upon the earth an hundred and fifty days. |
| *Fear of the Gods.* | | |
| 5 Even in Heaven the Gods feared the flood | | |
| 6 And sought refuge, they ascended to the Heaven of Anu | | |
| 7 The Gods like dogs in kennels lay in heaps | | And Elohim remembered Noah, and every living thing, and all the cattle that were with him in the ark ; |
| *Istar as the Divine Mother.* | | |
| 8 Then cried Istar like a Mother | | |
| 9 And the great Goddess does utter her speech | | |
| 10 All things to clay are turned | | |
| 11 And the evil which I proclaimed in the presence of the Gods | | |
| 12 As I announced in the presence of the Gods, is that evil | | |
| 13 As I announced to evil are devoted all my people | | |

P

## Hebrew Narrative—*cont.*

| Chaldean Deluge Tablet—*cont.* | Jehovistic Account. | Elohistic Account. |
|---|---|---|
| Line<br>14 And though I the Mother have begotten my people<br>15 Yet like the Spawn of fishes they fill the Sea<br>16 Then the Gods were weeping with her concerning the Spirits<br>17 The Gods on their thrones were seated weeping<br>18 Covered were their Lips because of the Coming Evil<br><br>*Duration of Rain.*<br><br>19 Six days and nights<br>20 The Wind, the Deluge and the Storm go on sweeping away<br>21 The seventh day when it approached the rain subsided, and the great Deluge<br>22 Which had assailed like a host<br>23 Was appeased. | And the rain was upon the earth forty days and forty nights. And the deluge was forty days upon the earth; and the waters increased, and bare up the ark, and it was lift up above the earth. And every living thing was destroyed which was upon the face of the ground, both man, and cattle and creeping thing and fowl of the heaven, and they were destroyed from the earth; and Noah only was left, and they that were with him in the ark. | And Elohim made a wind to pass over the earth and the waters assuaged ; |

| Chaldean Deluge Tablet—*cont.* | Hebrew Narrative—*cont.* | |
|---|---|---|
| | Jehovistic Account. | Elohistic Account. |
| *Cessation of Rain.*<br>Line<br>23   The Sea began to dry and the Wind and flood ended<br>24  I watched the Sea making a tossing<br>25  And the whole of Mankind had turned to clay<br>26  Like reeds the Corpses floated<br>27  I opened the Window and the light struck on my face<br>28  I was sad at Heart, I sat down, I wept<br>29  Over my face flowed my tears<br>30  I looked at the regions bounding the Sea<br>31  To the 12 points no land (was seen)<br><br>*The Ark rests on the Mountain.*<br>32  To the Country of Nizir floated the Ship<br>33  The Mountain of Nizir stopped the Ship and to pass o'er it was not able<br>34  The first day, the second day the Mountain of Nizir the same<br>35  The third day and fourth day the Mountain of Nizir the same | And the rain from heaven was restrained; and the waters returned from off the earth continually. | The fountains also of the deep and the flood-gates of heaven were stopped, and after the end of an hundred and fifty days the waters decreased. . . . And the waters decreased continually until the tenth month; in the tenth month, on the first day of the month, were the tops of the mountains seen. And it came to pass in the six hundred and first year, in the first month, the first day of the month, the waters were dried up from off the earth; and in the second month, on the seven and twentieth day of the month, was the earth dry.<br><br>And the ark rested in the seventh month on the seventeenth day of the month, upon the mountains of Ararat. |

| Chaldean Deluge Tablet—cont. | Hebrew Narrative—cont. | |
| --- | --- | --- |
| | JEHOVISTIC ACCOUNT. | ELOHISTIC ACCOUNT. |
| Line<br>36 The fifth and sixth day the Mountain of Nizir the same<br>37 On the seventh day in the course of it<br><br>*Sending forth the Dove.*<br><br>38 I sent forth the Dove, it left. The Dove went and turned<br>39 A resting place it saw not, it returned back | [And Noah stayed seven days] and he sent forth a dove from him to see if the waters were abated from off the face of the ground: but the dove found no rest for the sole of her foot, and she returned unto him to the ark, for the waters were on the face of the whole earth; and he put forth his hand and took her and brought her in unto him into the ark. And he stayed yet other seven days; and again he sent forth the dove out of the ark; and the dove came in to him at eventide; and lo, in her mouth a fresh olive-leaf pluckt off; so Noah knew that the waters were abated from off the earth. And he stayed yet other seven days; and sent forth the dove; and she returned not again to him any more | |

| Chaldean Deluge Tablet—cont. | Hebrew Narrative—cont. | |
|---|---|---|
| | Jehovistic Account. | Elohistic Account. |
| *Sending forth the Swallow.*<br>Line<br>40 I sent forth a Swallow, it left and turned and<br>41 A resting place it could not see, and it returned back | | |
| *Sending forth the Raven.*<br>42 I sent forth a Raven and it left<br>43 The Raven went and the Corpses (Carrion) which were on the Water it saw<br>44 It did eat—it floated and was carried away —it returned not | And it came to pass at the end of forty days that Noah opened the window of the ark which he had made, and he sent forth a raven, and it went forth to and fro, until the waters were dried up from off the earth. | |
| *The Coming forth from the Ark.*<br>45 I sent the (Animals) forth to the four Winds (of Heaven) | And Noah removed the covering of the ark, and looked, and behold, the face of the ground was dry | And Elohim spake unto Noah, saying: Go forth of the ark, thou and thy wife and thy sons, and thy son's wives with thee: Bring forth with thee every living thing that is with thee, of all flesh, both fowl and cattle, and every creeping thing that creepeth upon the earth; that they may breed abundantly in the earth and be |

| Chaldean Deluge Tablet—cont. | Hebrew Narrative—cont. | |
| --- | --- | --- |
| | Jehovistic Account. | Elohistic Account. |
| *The Sacrifice.* | | fruitful and multiply in the earth. And Noah went forth, and his sons, and his son's wives with him; every beast, every creeping thing, and every fowl, whatsoever moveth upon the earth, after their families, went forth out of the ark. |
| Line | | |
| 45  I sacrificed a Sacrifice | And Noah builded an altar unto Yahveh; and took of every clean beast, and of every clean fowl, and offered burnt offerings upon the altar. And Yahveh smelled the sweet savour; | |
| 46  I built the Altar on the peak of the Mountain | | |
| 47  Adgur Jars by sevens I placed | | |
| 48  Below them I spread reeds, pine wood and Spices | | |
| 49  The Gods smelled the Odour. The Gods smelled the Sweet Odour | | |
| 50  The Gods like flies over the Master the Sacrifice gathered | | |
| *The Rainbow.* | | |
| 51  Then from afar the great Goddess in her approach | | And Elohim said, This is the token of the covenant which I make between me and you and every living creature that is with you, for perpetual generations: I have set my bow in the cloud, and it |
| 52  Raised up the great zones which Anu had created as his glory | | |

## THE APPEASING OF BEL.

### Chaldean Deluge Tablet—cont.

#### COLUMN IV.

Line
1 Those days I had thought of and never may
   I forget them
2 May the Gods come to my Altar
3 May Bel not come to my Altar,
4 Since he did not reflect and make a deluge
5 And consigned my people to the deep
6 When thereupon Bel in his approach
7 Saw the Ship stopped. His Heart was filled
   with anger upon Gods and Spirits

### Hebrew Narrative—cont.

#### JEHOVISTIC ACCOUNT.

#### ELOHISTIC ACCOUNT.

shall be for a token of a covenant between me and the earth; and it shall come to pass when I bring a cloud over the earth, and the bow shall be seen in the cloud, and I will remember my covenant between me and you and every living creature of all flesh; and the waters shall no more become a deluge to destroy all flesh. And the bow shall be in the cloud: and I will look upon it, that I may remember the everlasting covenant between Elohim and every living creature of all flesh that is upon the earth.

| Chaldean Deluge Tablet—cont. | Hebrew Narrative—cont. | |
|---|---|---|
| | Jehovistic Account. | Elohistic Account. |
| *Council of the Gods.*<br>Line<br>8 Let none come forth alive. Let no man escape the deep<br>9 Adar opened his mouth and spake, he says to the Warrior Bel<br>10 Whosoever except Ea can make a design<br>11 Even Ea knows and all things he teaches<br>12 Ea opened his mouth and spake, he says to the Warrior Bel<br><br>*The Deluge a Punishment for Sin.*<br>13, 14 Oh! thou Counsellor of the Gods, Why, why didst thou reflect and didst make a Deluge<br>15 Let the doer of sin bear his sin and let the transgressor bear his transgression<br>16 May the Just Prince not be cut off, may the faithful not perish<br><br>*No more Deluge.*<br>17 Instead of making a deluge, may Lions increase and Men be decreased<br>18 Instead of making a deluge, may Jackals increase and Men be decreased<br>19 Instead of making a deluge, may Famine happen and Men be wasted | And Yahveh said in his heart, I will not again curse the ground any more for the sake of the man, for that the imagination of man's heart is evil from his youth; neither will | Neither shall all flesh be cut off any more by the waters of the deluge; neither shall there be any more a deluge to destroy the earth. |

| Chaldean Deluge Tablet—*cont.* | Hebrew Narrative—*cont.* | |
|---|---|---|
| | Jehovistic Account. | Elohistic Account. |
| Line | | |
| 20 Instead of making a deluge, may Pestilence increase and Men decrease | I again smite any more every living thing as I have done. | |
| 21 I did not reveal the hidden thing of the Gods | | |
| 22 To the Reverent and Wise One a dream I sent him and the hidden thing he heard | | |
| 23 When Bel had reflect on his Counsel he went up into the midst of the Ship | | |
| 24 He took my Hand and raised me up | | |
| 25 He caused me to rise up and placed my Wife by my side | | |
| *Covenant.* | | |
| 26 He turned himself to us and established himself to us in a Covenant. | While the earth remaineth, seed-time and harvest, and cold and heat, and summer and winter, and day and night shall not cease. | And Elohim spake unto Noah and to his sons with him, saying: And I, behold, I establish my covenant with you and with your seed after you; and with every living creature that is with you, the fowl, the cattle, and every beast of the earth with you: of all that go out of the ark, even every beast of the earth; and I will establish my covenant with you. |
| *Translation of the Hero.* | | |
| 27 Hitherto Samas-Napisti has been a mortal man | | |
| 28 Even now Samas-Napisti and his Wife are made like unto gods and borne away as | | |
| 29 Then shall dwell Samas-Napisti in a remote place at the Mouth of the Rivers | | |
| 30 They took us, and in a remote place at the Mouth of the Rivers they seated us | | |

This important inscription bears a close relationship to the tradition preserved by the Greco-Chaldean historian Berosos, which has been handed down to us in the writings of Josephus (*Cont. Apion*. i. 19). The discovery of this valuable record is most important, because it not only confirms the Greek version, but also establishes a closer harmony between the Hebrew and classical tradition, upon which the Hebrew historian Josephus relied. The tradition of Berosos is as follows :—" In this year the god Bel revealed to Xisuthrus, in a dream, that in the fifteenth year, in the month Daesius, there would be a great storm of rain, and men would be destroyed by the flood of waters. He bade him bury all written records,—the ancient, mediæval, and modern,—in Sippara, the city of the Sun, and build a ship and embark in it with his kindred and nearest friends. He was also to take food and drink into the ship, and carry into it all creatures, winged and four-footed. Xisuthrus did as he was bidden, and built a boat fifteen stadia long and two stadia in breadth, and placed in it his wife and child, relations, and friends. Then the inundation came. When the rain ceased Xisuthrus sent out some birds, but they returned back to the ship, as they could find nothing to eat and no place of rest. After a few days he sent out other birds. These also returned with mud on their feet. Then Xisuthrus sent yet others, and they never returned. Xisuthrus knew that the earth had appeared. He took out a part of the roof of his boat, and perceived that it had settled down on a mountain. Then he went out with his wife and daughter and the architect of the boat. He worshipped the earth and built an altar, offered sacrifice to the gods, and then disappeared, together with those whom he had brought out of the boat.

When his companions whom he had left in the boat had gone out, and were in search of Xisuthrus, his voice called to them out of the air, saying that the gods had carried him away in regard for his piety—that he, with his daughter and architect, were dwelling among the gods."

It is at once evident that there are many and striking resemblances between the Babylonian, the Greco-Babylonian, and the Hebrew records of this great cataclysm. Both the tradition and the tablet agree in attributing the Deluge to the god Bel. With regard to the Hebrew accounts it is clear that that of the Jehovistic writer presents a closer resemblance to the Assyrian version. This is especially to be noticed in the frequent use of the period of seven days (Gen. 7. 4.), in the downpour of rain (7. 12; 8. 2), the closing of the door of the ark (*ib.* 7. 16), the birds sent forth thrice (*ib.* 8. 8–12), the sacrifice after the ceasing of the flood and the pleasure of God at its sweet savour (*ib.* 8. 20); all constitute a close agreement, whereas the Elohistic version, with the exception of general features, there is hardly any other detailed agreement, with the exception of the passages relating to the building of the ark (*ib.* 6. 14–16). There are many points of resemblance which amount to most striking coincidences, as the use of the expression *Zir napisti buladh*, "preserve the seed of life" (i. 21), which reminds us at once of the Hebrew, "to preserve seed" (*ib.* 7. 3); and also all three accounts agree in the inclusion of "relatives" among the rescued (*ib.* 6. 18; 7. 7); in the inscription (col. ii. 29)—*Kala Kimti ya u nisati ya*, "all my family and relatives."

It has been asserted by several writers that the most important difference between the Babylonian and Hebrew records consists in the polytheistic elements in the former.

This, in the main, is perfectly correct; but when we carefully examine the documents, I maintain that the polytheistic element is not so real as it appears at first sight. Although the decision to destroy life by a deluge is arrived at by a council of the gods (col. i. 13), and in this the leading part seems to have been that of the god Bel (col. iv. 4), yet the position of the god Ea in the story has so remarkable a resemblance to that of Jehovah in the Hebrew, as to lead us to institute a much closer comparison than at first seemed possible.*

It is Ea who announces the coming of the deluge (col. i. 17), directs the building of the ark (col. i. 24–27), announces the period of entry and closing of the door (col. i. 39, 40; ii. 34), intercedes for man with the offended Bel (col. iv. 12–20), and finally the Chaldean sage is translated, like Enoch, to dwell in the specially sacred region of Ea, at the mouth of the rivers (col. iv. 29). Thus it will be seen how closely the position of Ea resembles that of Jehovah. He was the lord of the city of Surippak, "the ark city," and Samas-Napisti always addresses him as "Ea, my lord." So that, although there is a polytheistic element, there is at the same time a curious unity in the relationship of Ea to the cataclysm.

In the same manner there seems to be a direct inference that the Deluge was a punishment for sin decreed by the gods. In the first portion we read, "Every one who has turned from me shall be punished, for the protection of the gods is over me;" and this is more emphatically brought out in the subsequent phrase (col. iv. 13, 14). This phrase is so remarkable that it needs a further comment—*atta malik ilani kuradu ki, ki, la tamtalikma abbub taskun*—"And

---

* Schrader, *Cuneiform Insc. and the Old Test.*, p. 49.

thou warrior, counsellor of the gods, why? why? didst thou not consider, and didst make a deluge?" *Bēl khite emid khita su, bel gillati emid gillat su*—" Let the doer of sin bear his sin ; let the blasphemer bear his blasphemy."

We then have the plea of Ea, that in place of the Deluge there would be substituted the destroying forces of nature:—

> Instead of making a deluge may lions increase and men be decreased;
> Instead of making a deluge may jackals increase and men be decreased;
> Instead of making a deluge may famine (*Khusakhu*) be established (and men decrease);
> Instead of making a deluge may pestilence (*dibbara*) be established and men decrease.

In this passage the dreaded trinity of destruction—plague, pestilence, and famine—is vividly described in similar language to that used in the Scriptures; for example, "I will consume them by the sword, and by the famine, and by the pestilence" (Jer. **14.** 12; **27.** 13); and again, in the choice of the visitants to diminish the people of Israel after the numbering by David (2 Sam. **24.** 15). Both the lion (*nesu*) and the jackal (*akhu*) were the emblems of the dread god of death. The jackal, as in the case of the emblem of Anubis in Egypt, was chosen on account of his association with the graveyard. By the Akkadians it was called LIK BARRA, "the Evil dog"; by the Semites *Akhu*, "the Evil One"; the *Okhim*, "doleful creatures." (Isa. **13.** 21), of the Bible. Upon a boundary stone of the twelfth century B.C. the jackal is represented as the emblem of Nergal, the god of death ; and in the palace of Khorsabad a small statue,

134    THE SHIP OF EA AND THE ARK.

a "teraphim figure," of the god of death, with a jackal's head, was found.*

The death-dealing character of the Deluge is well conveyed in the words put into the mouth of the great goddess Istar:—" Then cried Istar like a bearing mother (*alidat*), uttered the great goddess her speech. All things this day to clay are turned—like the spawn of fishes (*abli·nuni*) they fill the sea" (col. iii. 9, 10, 15), and "All mankind to clay had turned, like reeds the corpses floated." So that the utter destruction of all is clearly indicated.

**The Ark.**—The ark of the Assyrian account differs very much from that of the Hebrew accounts, being clearly a ship, while the Hebrew תֵּבָה, *tebah*, is a box or large receptacle, with no resemblance to a ship. The directions given for the construction of the ark are most minute, and it is very unfortunate that the portions relating to the size are lost. In its details the Elohistic version (Gen. 6. 14)† approaches nearer the Chaldean and also the tradition of Berosos, who assigns to the ark the immense size of fifteen stadia in length and two in breadth, while the Hebrew dimensions are three hundred cubits in length, fifty in breadth, and thirty in height (*ib.* 6. 15).‡ The description of the ark in the inscription seems to be based upon that

---

\* See Boscawen, *Dust of Ages*, p. 126.
† In the detailed descriptions with which the Elohistic writer supplements his descriptions, it is important to notice the resemblance they bear to the Babylonian text. The use of bitumen (6. 14), the attempt to specify the proportions of the ark (6. 15), the rainbow (9. 13). The numbers employed are also curiously Babylonian. The age of Noah, 600 years, is the Babylonian *ner*, while 40 is the sacred number of the god Ea, and 7 was sacred alike to Babylonians and Hebrews. Upon these numbers see Schrader, *Cuneiform Insc. and the Old Test.*, p. 49.
‡ It will be remembered that the word *tebah* is used for the bulrush ark of Moses (Exod. 2. 5), and upon this ground Schrader (p. 53) is inclined to connect the word with the Egyptian *teb*, a box. This seems to me hardly proved. It may be, perhaps, a survival of the *basket of rushes*, in which Sargon, of Akkad, the great hero king of the Semites, was placed (W. A. I., iii., 4. 7).

JACKAL-HEADED GOD.
(*Photographed from the original.*)

of the sacred ship of Ea, which is described in one of the hymns of Eridu :—

### THE SHIP OF EA.

Its helm is of cedar wood;
Its serpent-like oar has a handle of gold ;
Its mast is capped with the turquoise stone ;
Seven times seven lions of the desert hold its deck ;*
The god Adar fills its cabin within ;
Its planks are the cedar of the forest ;
Its covering is the palm of Dilmun ;†
Carry away its heart is the channel ;
Making glad its heart is the sun rise ;
Its house, its stair, is a mountain that gives rest to the heart ;
The Ship of Ea is the (ship) of Fate ; ‡
Ningal the princess is the goddess whose word is life ;
Merodach is the god who utters the holy name.§

**Provisioning the Ark.**—In this passage considerably more detail is given in the tablet than in the Hebrew account; but, again, there is a distinct variation between the Jehovist and the Elohist. The former inserts the division of clean and unclean animals. As in the Creation Tablets, a clear distinction is made between the domestic and wild animals. The line reads, *būl zeri umam zeri* .... *kali sunu useli*, "Cattle of the field, wild animals of the field .... all of them I caused to go up" (col. ii. 29). In the account of Berosos the express command is made to take provisions; and in the tablet we read, "Wine and oil, drinks I placed within it like the waters of a river, even as for a feast-day" (col. ii. 17-19).

---

* Compare the lions on the throne of Solomon in Talmudic and Arab legends.
† The islands of Bahrein, in the Persian Gulf.
‡ This might well be a name of the ark.
§ In a hymn to Merodach (W. A. I., iv., 20. 1) we read *Ivat baladhu kūvu*, "The breath (that gives) life is thine"; and *Sipat baladhu kūvu*, "The word (that gives) life *is* thine."

The Deluge.—The description which the tablet gives of the great storm is grand in the extreme. In the first place a definite season is fixed for its commencement—" the season (*adan*) which the Sun-god had fixed " (col. ii. 30). That season (*adanna su*) drew near: " Went forth the cry in the night, I will cause it to rain from heaven heavily " (*šamūt kibāti*). This season was evidently that which has already been described in the chapter on the Creation Tablets as extending from the 1st *Kisleu* (Nov.-Dec.) to the 30th day of *Sebat* (Jan.-Feb.), when the sun is in the (*kisadi*) course of Ea, the season of storms (*urpati*). The period embraced the terrible month *Iti-aša Segi*, "the month of the curse of rain"—the *Sabatu*, or "month of destruction," of the Semitic calendar. This was the eleventh month of the year, and came under the zodiac sign of Aquarius. It was evidently the dread winter season called *Kharpu*, the Hebrew חֹרֶף, which is explained by the groups meaning "crops are (in) future," that is, the sowing season. These definite statements serve to show that the Babylonian legend was based upon a definite climatological theory.

These three months of the winter season were respectively called *Id Abba-E*, " the month of the going forth of the sea "—the *Tebitu*, or " month of the inundation," of the Semitic calendar; the month of *Sebat*, which we have already explained; and the month called *Id-gan-gana*, the " month of clouds "—the *Kislevu*, or " strong month " of the Semites.

The Deluge, then, took place at the culmination of the stormy season. Of the character of this period of the year there is ancient evidence. Sennacherib says: " The advance I ordered in the month Tebit, a terrible storm arose, and heaven and earth it flooded ; rains upon rain, and snow the

HYMNS OF THE STORM GODS. 137

channels filled." In the same manner in the annals of Esarhaddon we read, "Snow storming in the month Sebat came; the mighty darkness I feared not." It is, then, to this period of the year that the great storm is assigned. The description of the storm is exactly that of one of the terrible winter storms of the Mesopotamian valley,\* all the destroying powers of nature being let loose.

  Then arose the water of dawn at daylight;
  It arose up like a black cloud (*urpatam zalamtum*) from the horizon of heaven;†
  The Thunder-god (Rimmon) in the midst of it thundered;
  Nebo and the Wind-god ‡ march in front;
  The throne bearers (*Guzalli*) § traverse mountain and plain;
  The Pestilence-god (*Dibbara*) ‖ brings with him affliction;
  The War-god (*Ninip*) in front casts down.
  The Angels of Earth (*Annunaki*) bear flaming brands; ¶
  In their wild course they burn up the earth;
  The deluge of the Rain-god reaches to heaven; \*\*
  All that is visible to darkness †† is turned.

This is one of the most finished pieces of Assyrian writing, and probably represents the highest form of the tradition.

---

 \* See *Dust of Ages*, p. 177.
 † We may compare this rising of the storm with that of the rain in answer to the prayer of Elijah (1 Kings 18). The rapid rise of storms in the East is well known.
 ‡ *Sar*, "the Wind-god," the Hebrew שְׂאוּר.
 § The *Guzalli*, or throne-bearers, are manifestly the storm-clouds, and the passage calls to mind the Hebrew words, "He did fly upon the wings of the wind" (Ps. 18. 10). The *Guzalli* are also the mysterious composite figures who support the seats of the gods, like the cherubim, as represented on the Sun-god tablet from Sippara in the British Museum.
 ‖ *Dibbara*, the Hebrew דֶּבֶר, *Deber*, "the pestilence." We may compare these lines with those of the prophet Habbakuk, "Before him went the pestilence, and the fever burned before his feet" (Hab. 3. 5).
 ¶ *Dibrati*, a doubtful word; "flaming brands," perhaps "the lightning."
 \*\* The full height of the Deluge is called in the inscription *Pul abubi*, "the heap of the Deluge."
 †† The word *etute*, of which the root is עָטָה, means "a thick, impenetrable darkness," such as that in Egypt. The word is used in the Istar Tablet for the darkness of Sheol, or the "House of Death." *Nuru ul imiru ina etute alba*, "Light they see not, in thick darkness they sit."

R

There are, however, traces of an older tradition preserved in a few fragments; as, for example,—

The tempest from the midst of space (*absu*)
The fatal decree (*Mamit*) from the midst of Heaven proceeds.
It sweeps the earth as the verdure is swept;
To the four winds its terror spreads like fire.
To the men of the habited earth it causes affliction to their body.
In the city and the country it causes destruction to small and great;
Strong one and menial bewail it.
In the heavens and earth like a water-spout it pours down rain.
To the holy place of their god they hasten and cry aloud.

This fragment appears, as already stated, to contain some traces of an older tradition, and no doubt from time to time other portions of the same nature will be recovered. Many of these, no doubt, referred to local floods, but they show the class of literature that preceded the composition of the epic.

Another fragment, which seems to be of the same class, is as follows (W. A. I., 27. 5):—

Like a cup of wine (*karpat karani*) poured out [it is] upon them.
Country unto country looks afraid;
The female servant to her chamber flees upward;
The head of the house by the entrance of the house it ushers forth;
The son of the house from the house of his father it drives forth;
The doves (*sumati*) in their cotes it takes;
The bird on its wing it caused to mount upward;
The swallow (*sinuntu*) in its nest (*kini*) it caused to fly;
The ox it struck down, the young ass it smote;
Great dragons, evil spirits, were their huntsmen.

*Note.*—It is particularly interesting here in this fragment to see the dove and the swallow associated with the day of evil, as it certainly prepares us for their appearance in the older legend.

**Resting Place of the Ark.**—Here again there is a marked difference. The Jehovistic writer leaves the resting place unnamed, while the Elohistic (Gen. 8. 4) specifies it as the mountain of Ararat (אֲרָרָט)—the region of Armenia—and the tablet specifies distinctly the mountain of Nizir, a district whose situation can be easily established by the historical inscriptions. Upon this subject much light has been thrown during recent years by the inscriptions, and especially by Professor Sayce in his able treatise on the cuneiform inscription from Van in Armenia.*

According to the Hebrew record the Ark rested on Mount Ararat. This is the land of Uradhu of the inscriptions, and embraces all the plain and basin of the Araxes, to the north-east of Assyria, a district which corresponds very closely with the Nizir of the inscriptions.

The position of this latter district is fixed by the inscriptions of Assur-nazir-pal (B.C. 885), who says that he marched from Kalzu near Arbela to the towns of Baisti and Babiti in the land of Nizir. This fixes the district in the table land of Pamir, a little south of Mount Rowandiz. There is a very widespread and ancient tradition that it was on Jebel Gudi—Mount Gudi—that the Ark rested. This Gudi is manifestly the Gute or Kute of the inscriptions—the land of the Goim (גּוֹיִם) of the Hebrews—the district to the north-east of Babylonia, where dwelt the *zabmanda* or nomad barbarians who from time to time swept over Western Asia, a region regarded of old time as the womb of nations, and therefore a fit site for the Mountain of the Nations. Upon a valuable astronomical tablet it is stated that the region to the east of Babylonia—that is, north-east—is that of Suedin and Guti; that is, the mountain range of Pamir and the plain watered by the Zab and

---

* *Jour. R.A.S.*, vol. xiv., New Series, pt. 3.

the Tornadus. This is evidently the district referred to by the writer of Isa. 14. 13, who describes the king of Babylon as boasting he "will ascend into heaven, and exalt his throne above the stars of the gods," and "will sit on the mountain of the assembly of the gods in the extremities of the north." It was therefore in this region that the Babylonians placed the resting-place of the Ark. This position agrees exactly with that ascribed to the resting-place of the Ark according to Berosos, who says, "On the Gordyæan Mountains, where it is settled, remains of the boat of Xisuthrus were in existence for a long time after." It was in memory of the resting-place that the Babylonians built temples called *Kharsag Kalama*, "Mountain of the Nations," and *Kharsag Kurra*, "Mountain of the East."

The district of *Uradhu*, Ararat, or Armenia, lay immediately adjoining this on the north, and may, no doubt, at the time of the Elohistic writer have embraced the traditional resting-place. The divergence between the Babylonian tablet, the Hebrew account, and the tradition of Berosos is not so great as at first appears, and it must be borne in mind that the Elohistic writer is by no means explicit in his expression "a mountain of Ararat."

"**Sending forth the Birds.**"—This incident is common to all three accounts, but while the Greco-Chaldean version simply mentions birds, the tablet and the Hebrew version specify the birds, and the order of their despatch. In the tablet the order is dove, swallow, raven. In the Hebrew account the swallow is not mentioned, the dove is sent forth twice, and the raven is sent forth first instead of last (Gen. 8. 6-12), and no such explicit reason for his non-return is afforded us in the tablet (col. iii. 42-44) : "The raven went, and it left; the raven went, the carrion of the waters it saw. It did eat, it floated, and was carried away; it returned not." In the Hebrew account also the dove is sent forth a fourth time, not to return (Gen. 8. 13). In this respect, as indicated by Schrader, the tablet exhibits a much more systematic sequence of thought than that of the Hebrew writer.\*

Omens in Babylonia were frequently derived from the flight of birds.† The choice of the swallow is easily to be explained, as in Akkadian it was called *simkhu*, " the destiny bird," omens, no doubt, being derived from the direction of its beautiful gyrations of flight.

**The Sacrifice of Thanksgiving.**—Here again is found a remarkable detailed agreement with the Hebrew: "And Noah built an altar unto Jehovah, and took of every clean beast and of every clean bird, and offered burnt offerings upon the altar, and Jehovah smelled the sweet savour." As in other passages, the tablet presents considerably more detail: "I sacrificed a sacrifice, I built an altar on the peak of a mountain. *Adyur* jars by sevens I placed; below them I spread reeds, pine wood, and spices; the gods smelled the odour, the gods smelled the sweet savour.‡ The gods like flies over the master of the sacrifice gathered."

**The Rainbow.**—This particular token of the covenant occurs only in the Elohistic account, and the words are very remarkable: "My bow I have set in the cloud, and it shall be for a token of a covenant between me and the

---

\* See his important remark in *Cuneiform Insc. and the Old Test.*, pp. 50–53.

† See Mr. Pinches' paper on the *Surdu* bird (falcon or hawk) in *Proc. Soc. Bib. Arch.*, vol. vi., p. 212.

‡ The passage reads as follows: *Ilani izinu irisa, Ilani izinu irisa tabu.* "The gods smelled the savour, the gods smelled the sweet savour."

earth. And it shall come to pass, when I bring a cloud over the earth, that the bow shall be seen in the cloud" (Gen. 9. 13, 14). There is no trace of this in the Greek tradition of Berosos. In the tablet, however, a most interesting passage is given which relates to this divine bow: *Ultu ulanum-ma Istar ina Kasadi-su issi namzabi\* rabati sa Anum ipusu ki zukhi-su*, "From afar Istar in her approach lifted up the great arches which Anu had made for his glory." There can be no doubt as to the meaning of this passage, and the bow of the Deluge is again distinctly mentioned in a hymn (W. A. I., ii., 19. 7, 8), where *gis-bam matu* is explained by *Kistu abubi*, "the bow of the Deluge," the Hebrew קֶשֶׁת (Gen. 9. 13).

**Translation of Samas-Napisti.**—The covenant having been completed and ratified by the sign of the rainbow, the reward of the faithful one is forthcoming. The tablet reads, "Hitherto Samas-Napisti has been a mortal man. Even now Samas-Napisti and his wife are made like unto gods and borne away. Then shall dwell Samas-Napisti

---

\* In the Assyrian syllabary there are two signs which very closely resemble each other, namely, ⟨⟩ and ⟨⟩. The former is the one used here, and we find it explained in the syllabaries by *saku*, "high"; *elamu*, "Elam," or "Highland"; by *Šamû*, "heaven," and by *nakaru ša šemiri*, "boring (קְבִי) of the diamond" (שָׁמִיר) (Jer. 17. 1; Ezek. 3. 9), and then also by the words *namzabu*. This last word is evidently the well-known Hebrew word (מַצֵּבָה) *mazebah*, "a stone pillar," especially one set up as by Jacob at Bethel (Gen. 28. 18), as the mark of a covenant between himself and God. In this respect the rainbow may have been regarded as a species of divine pillars or *mazebahs*, set up by the lord of heaven, and in this we may see the idea of the sign of the covenant. This seems to be borne out by the next line of the inscription, which would be unintelligible were it not for the association with the "stones of covenant,"—*Ilani annuti lu aban ukni irtiya at amsi*: "Those gods by the stone on my breast may I never forget." This stone was probably one of the small conical miniature *mazebahs* worn on the neck as a talisman, and by which oaths were sworn, and which ranked in equal importance with the signet seal. The second sign is explained by *kastu* (קֶשֶׁת) and *midpanu*, "the bow," and is evidently in the archaic form a rude picture of the bow and arrow.

SEAL REPRESENTING CHALDEAN NOAH.
(Photographed from the original.)

in a remote place at the mouth of the rivers." Of this translation no trace is found in the Hebrew narrative. According to the Biblical account Noah died at the age of 950 years. While the translation of the Chaldean sage seems to find a parallel in the pious Enoch, who was translated at the age of 365 years. It is important to notice that Berosos preserves the tradition in the words, "When his companions whom he had left in the boat had gone out, and were in search of Xisuthrus, his voice called to them out of the air, saying that the gods had carried him away in regard for his piety." As became one so directly associated with Ea, the god of the sea, his home was placed at the mouth of the rivers, a region considered especially sacred.

**The Names Samas-Napisti, Xisuthrus, and Noah.**—One point which would at the outset strike the reader is the great difference in the names of the heroes of the three traditions of the Epic, but a little consideration will reveal that there is a reason for each and a certain relationship between all three. The name used in the Epic, *Samas-napisti*, the "Living Sun," is one used in contrast to that of the hero Gilgames, or Nimrod. He is the sick, dying winter sun, shorn of his locks and afflicted with leprosy, who goes each year to inquire the secret of healing and immortality from the "Living Sun." It is the contrast between these two which forms the *raison d'être* of the story being woven into the Epic.

The epithets applied to the translated sage are very important. He is spoken of as *Adra-Khassis*, "Reverent" and "Wise," a name which Mr. George Smith thought formed the basis of the Xisuthrus (*Khasis-adra*) of Berosos;

but this is no longer admitted. The name Xisuthrus is manifestly a corruption of *Zi Susru*, "spirit of the founder," afterwards at a late harmonising period adopted as one of the titles of Anu, the god of Heaven. The most important epithet, however, is one frequently applied to the sage—*Samas-napisti rukuti*. Samas-napisti, the far-distant, remote or ancient one. The importance of this name is in the relationship which seems to exist between it and that of Noah. The name Noah is generally connected with the root *nukh*, נוח, and rendered "Rest," a meaning that seems to have no direct relationship to the life of the patriarch. If, however, the name, as Goldziher and others have suggested, is connected with the Ethiopic *nukh*, "long-lived, ancient," it forms a curious parallel to the Babylonian epithet *rukuti*. In Arabic and Ethiopic tradition the life of Noah was a bye-word. "A life like that of Nukh" being almost synonymous with immortality.

We have now completed our study of this remarkable and priceless document. Of its direct relationship to the Hebrew account there can be little doubt, but it is sufficiently distinct to mark it as a separate version. With regard to any contact between the two traditions the same remarks apply to the Deluge Tablets as already applied to the Creation Tablets; both formed part of Babylonian literature as early as B.C. 2000, and must have been accessible. It is premature in the light of recent discovery, even if it were possible, to pronounce any distinct opinion as to the contacts between the Hebrew and Chaldean. It may be concluded that there was an almost universal tradition among the ancient people of Western Asia of this great cataclysm, and that the various traditions have many and striking points of agreement, with local and religious differences.

## CHAPTER VI.

### THE GRAVE AND THE FUTURE STATE.

IN the study of the religious life and literature of an ancient people, no section is more important than that of eschatology, or the beliefs which *they* held regarding the future state.

Fascinating as the subject is, it at the same time often presents very great difficulty. This is not so much owing to the paucity as to a superfluity of material and to a confusion of theories, the products of different schools of priestly teaching in the various ages.

In Egypt, that wonderful *magnum opus* of eschatological teaching, the so-called "Book of the Dead," or rather the book of the "Coming forth by Day,"* and the Pyramid Texts, show that not only was the theory of a future state deeply studied, but that it had assumed literary and to a certain extent, classical form at a very remote period. Complex and mystical, full of passages and symbols whose esoteric meanings were known only to the priests, the "Book of the Dead" may be said to have for all time constituted the whole teaching of the Egyptian priests as to a life after death.

Stereotyped as it became to a certain extent in very early ages, it was nevertheless a work which contained many

---

* The title of this work was *per em hru* "Coming forth by Day," and it must be of great antiquity, as copies of it have been discovered as early as in the XIIth Dynasty, B.C. 2500, and many chapters are attributed to the almost mythical ages of the Ist Dynasty (see Budge, *Nile*, pp. 9-10).

and varied component elements and not a few traces of the beliefs of the aboriginal Negro population whom the dynastic white Egyptians had replaced in the Nile valley.

The prominent place assigned to mystic animals—the apes (*Cynocephalus*), hippopotamus, the crocodile,—the transmigration of the soul through various animal forms, the use of magical knowledge and "words of power," all show that as the new comers from the Holy Land of Punt, *i.e.* S.E. Arabia, had inherited from them the worship of sacred animals in the various nomes, so the same influence had largely asserted itself in the eschatology of the "Book of the Dead."

The recent discoveries of Professor Petrie at Koptos have shown that while animal worship was not unknown to the Egyptian colonists who had entered the Nile valley at some remote period, their sacred animals were not those of the "Book of the Dead." Among them were the lion, the elephant, the gazelle, the bull, and the ostrich, such as have no place in the "Book of the Dead."

If we encounter a certain complexity in the Egyptian "Ritual of the Dead," when we come to study the theories of the future state taught in Babylonia, we encounter a far more confused mass of ideas.

Such a confusion is naturally to be expected in a community composed of so many mixed nationalities, who possessed so many different centres of religious teaching, complicated in later ages by borrowings from foreign sources. It is, however, to the complexity of Babylonian eschatological literature that we are compensated by the large mass of literature to which we have access, and the rich and varied illustrations of Biblical passages which may be gathered from them.

In examining the theories of such ancient schools of teaching as those of Eridu, Nipur, and Kutha, it is impossible to form any general conception of the Chaldeans regarding the "Future life." It will therefore be desirable to examine each in turn before arriving at any definite conclusions.

TEACHING OF ERIDU.

The most ancient and the most sacred city of Chaldea was the city of "*Eri-dugga*," the holy city, the Eridu of the Semites. It was to the religion of Babylonia what Jerusalem was to the Jews, or Amritza to the Brahmins. Situated in ancient times on the shores of the Persian Gulf, it was the seat of the worship of the Ocean-god Ea and his equally holy son, "Silik mulu-dugga," or Merodach, "the protector of good men."

In this city there had developed a wonderful creed of Religio-Magic, the product of the party minds of the Akkadians, to whom we are indebted for the earliest religious literature. The system revealed in the literature of Eridu, of which fortunately a great many tablets have been preserved, is that of a species of Shamanism. It can hardly in its earliest stages be dignified with the name of a religion, its main features being those of the animism of the Australian and American medicine-man.

In this cultus will be observed a simple belief in a soul in every thing. Every object in Nature owed its existence or being to an indwelling *life* or soul, similar to that which primitive man had satisfied himself was the source of his own vitality. The growing tree, the running river, the dark storm-cloud, or the sky-traversing sun, the wandering moon, the clustering stars, the blazing flame,—

each and all owed its being to an indwelling spirit. There was no moral element; all was due to the determination of chance. It was a religion of man's defence in his war with the powers of Nature and against his foes. Such a belief could have no priesthood who, by heart-stirring prayers, or fervent litanies, could appeal to man's better nature or love of the gods. It was only those who knew the mystic spells, the charms, the incantations which could exorcise, or ward off, or compel service from those terrible "spirits," who could aid man. There was therefore no such thing as a priesthood, only a caste of "medicine men," exorcists, and "witches," who professed to control or direct these spiritual powers.

To enter fully into the study of so complicated a system is beyond the scope of this chapter; but as an example of the confused nature of the literature of this creed, the following paragraphs may be quoted:—*

"The evil god, the evil demon, the demon of the field (plain), the demon of the mountain, the demon of the sea, the demon of the tomb, the evil spirit, the dazzling fiend, the evil wind, the assaulting wind which strips off the clothing of the body like an evil demon,—Conjure, O Spirit of Heaven; conjure, O Spirit of Earth!

"The sickness of the entrails, a sick heart, faintness of the heart, disease, disease of bile, headache, violent vomiting, a broken blood vessel, disease of the kidneys, painful disease which cannot be removed, a dream of ill omen,—Conjure, O Spirit of Heaven; conjure, O Spirit of Earth!

"Him who is the possessor of the likeness of another, the evil face, the evil eye, the evil tongue, the evil lips, the evil breath,—Conjure, O Spirit of Heaven; conjure, O Spirit of Earth!"

The above extract, from one of the earliest discovered Tablets, clearly shows the nature of the inscriptions and the form of belief they represent.

---

* See Sayce, *Hibbert Lectures*, p. 332.

Man is constantly in fear of the powers of Nature, the evil demons that produce disease and sickness, and of his fellow men; the baneful influence of each demon requires the protection of the exorcist.

Even in this fragment there is not, although it can be traced, the most primitive form; already an advance has been made. The fruit-giving Earth and the rain-giving Sky are regarded as good and mighty spirits who can control the opposing powers. Gradually the controlling spirits of Heaven and Earth come to be regarded as the creators of Heaven and Earth, and the lesser spirits as the inhabitants of these realms.

Thus may be seen the first conception of gods in this primitive belief. That it was the case is shown by the word for *god*.

The Akkadian word for god was *dimer* or *dimera*, with its dialectic variant *dinger* or *dingira*, derived from the root *dim*, "to create," or, "make" a synonym of the Semitic *banu*, *epišu*, *basu*, " to form," " to make," " to be."

In such a primitive creed as this it is evident that there could be no elaborate conception of the future life, as there was probably no idea of it.

The spirit of life, the indwelling *zi*, was partially absent in sleep, longer so in a trance, but came back on waking, or by the incantations of the Shaman; but in death it abandoned the body altogether, and could not be charmed back by the magician.

The bilingual tablets and syllabaries afford us many explanations of the important word *zi*, round which all this magic turns. It is explained by the word *napistu*, "life, soul," the Hebrew *nephesh*, which conveys an idea with which we are familiar in Hebrew literature, as in the words, "And the LORD formed man of the dust of the ground, and breathed into his nostrils the breath of life" (Gen. 2. 7). So also it may be explained by *kaṡu*, "double," a word which recalls the Greek conception of the *eidolon* and the Egyptian *ka*, or "double," the "genius" as distinct from the *ba* or soul.*

Another meaning attached to the word at a later period was that of *niṡu*, "spirit," or, as M. Lenormant has shown, "ghost," *niṡu* meaning "feeble." This word is a synonym of *tarpu*, "weak," from *rapu*, the Hebrew *Rephaim*, the "shades of the dead."†

In the same way, the word for death and corpse, *bad*, like the Semitic *mutu moth*, as Dr. Wright has shown,‡ means "to stretch oneself out," "extending"—an idea common alike to sleep and death. So also *pagru* (Heb. *peger*), "corpse," has a similar meaning.

In this creed there was no idea of a future state or of immortality; it had no place. The body from which the soul had departed might be brought back to life, but that only on this earth; and this act could only be performed by the great magician, "Silik-mulu-dugga," or Merodach, who knew the charm which gave life.

In a hymn to this deity which I have already quoted, a passage occurs which by many is regarded as implying a belief in immortality:—

> The incantation which gives life is thine,
> The breath (*ivat*) that gives life is thine.
> The holy writing of the mouth of the deep is thine.

Here, however, the office of the god is plainly that of the great magician, who by spell and incantation restores

---
\* See Maspero, on the *Ka*, in the *Trans. Soc. Bib. Arch.*, vol. viii., p. 142.
† See Sayce, *Hibbert Lectures*, p. 143.
‡ See *Trans. Soc. Bib. Arch.*, vol. iii., p. 107.

the dead to life, but in no way raises them to a place of immortality.

In the much later literature, such as the Cylinder of Cyrus, Merodach is spoken of as the "god who in his ministry raises the dead to life," but it must be borne in mind that such a belief, after many centuries of development, is produced by contact with other creeds.

## The Ghost Theory.

Besides the theory of animism, that is, the belief in countless spirits inhabiting all things in Nature, there is another theory which has often tended to produce the first steps in religious development. This is known as the "Ghost theory." In dreams, the primitive Akkadian, no doubt, imagined he saw the shadowy forms of his departed friends, which led him to regard them as not utterly vanished, but still existing as shades in some dark, far-distant, subterranean place.

Thus may be regarded the development of the idea of a ghost-world, presided over by a ghost-king and his consort. This ghost-god was called *Mullil*, or *Enlil*, "the lord of the ghost-world," and his wife, *Nin lil*, "lady of the ghost-world." The word *lil*, "a ghost," also meant "a dust cloud," to which the shadowy forms of ghosts were compared; it is also explained by *zakiku*, "transparent," "crystal": compare the Hebrew זְכוּכִית (*zekukith*) "crystal." The Akkadian *lil*, however, passed into Semitic Babylonian in the form of *lilum*, "ghost," with a feminine *litatum*, "the female ghost," "the night demon," "the vampire." This form was not unknown to the Hebrews, for Isaiah foretells the haunting of Idumea by the *Lilith* (Isa. 34. 14), while the Rabbis said that Adam had as his first wife a beautiful female named Lilith, who lived on the blood of children whom she slew at night.

The sacred city of the ghost-god was the city of Nipur, in Central South Babylonia, the site being marked by the mounds of Nuffar, recently explored by the American expedition from the University of Pennsylvania. This city was dedicated to the ghost-god, whose name occurs on all the bricks and inscriptions found there. There is an inscription of Sargon I., the king of Akkad, which belongs to the remote period of B.C. 3800, as follows: "To Mullil, the great lord, Sargani (Sargon), the king of the city, the mighty king, king of Akkad, the builder of the temple, the house of Mullil, in Nipur. Whosoever this tablet shall remove, Mullil and the Sun-god and the Goddess (Istar) his foundation shall tear up, and his seed obliterate." From the same site come inscriptions of the King Naram-Sin (Beloved of the Moon), reading "Naram Sin, the builder of the House of Mullil," and of Alušaršid, an hitherto unknown king of this dynasty. The latter reads "To Mullil Alušaršid, king of (the city of) Kiš, gave." These inscriptions show plainly that the worship of the "ghost-god" was fully established as early as B.C. 3800.

Another inscription from this city supplies further information with regard to this peculiar worship. It is inscribed upon a block of *lapis lazuli*, by order of the Kassite king, Kadašman-Tergu, who reigned about B.C. 1380. The opening lines only are of importance: "To Mullil of Nipur, father of the gods, king of the great Anunas, king of the World; his king, Kadašman-Turgu, king of Babylon (gave)."

## THE CHIEF ONES OF THE EARTH. 153

With the mention of the Anunas the first knowledge of any Chaldean idea of the future state is acquired. The word Anuna signifies the "master," or "great one," and corresponds to "the chief ones of the earth" (*alim*) of Isa. 14. 9. The Anunas, who dwelt in the realm of Mullil, were called the Anunage, or "Masters of the Under-world." They sat on golden thrones beside the stream of the "waters of life," in a land of darkness and decay.

Although seated on golden thrones in the dark underworld, there does not seem to be any indication of a belief in their future resurrection to life.

A great change however came over the eschatology of Babylonia, at what period is impossible to say, when the creed of Eridu, with its "ocean-god," and that of Nipur, with the worship of the "ghost-god," were blended together, and a third element was added, viz., that of the "Mountain of the World," where the gods met as on Olympus, and in the subterranean recesses of which was the land of Arallu, "the house of Death." This combination must have taken place very early, for in the inscriptions of Urbahu and Gudea, B.C. 2800, the "Lady of the Mountain of the World" is frequently mentioned. In the statue of the king Urbahu the inscription reads, "For the goddess Nin-garsag (Lady of the Mountains), mother of the gods." It is probably to this form of the myth which the Prophet Isaiah refers in the words: "I will ascend into heaven, I will exalt my throne above the stars of God, and sit upon the mountain of the congregation in the uttermost parts of the North" (Isa. 13. 13). The "Mountain of the World" and the mountain on which the Ark rested, Mount Nizir, were evidently closely related,

T

and were both the outcome of the early traditions of the old Akkadian mountain population who had come to settle in the plains of Shinar.

The nature of this mountain is well shown in the following hymn :—

> O mighty mountain of Mullil Im Kharsag (the sky mountain), whose head rivals the heavens, the pure deep is laid at its foundations.
> Among the mountains it couches as a strong bull,
> Its peaks glisten like the Sun-god;
> Like the star of heaven that proclaims the day, it is full of glittering rays.
> The mighty Mother Ninlil (the lady of the ghost world), the reverence of E Sara (the house of the host of heaven), the glory of E Kura (the temple of the host of earth), the adornment of E Giguna (the temple of darkness), the heart of the temple Ki-gusura (the temple of the land of light).*

The conception of this Chaldean Olympus is clearly seen in these lines. On the summit was the place of the Assembly of the gods, with the "temples of place of light," and "the house of the host of Heaven." In the interior was the abode of the Anunas, "the host of earth," and their meeting place, "the temple of Darkness."

This mythological topography exactly fits the description of Sheol given by the prophet Isaiah in his denunciation of Babylon (Isa. 14. 9, 15 ff.). It is impossible to read these verses in the light of cuneiform decipherment and not conclude that the writer was intimately acquainted with the main features of the Babylonian myths of the "World Mountain," the meeting place of the gods, and in whose interior was the ghost-kingdom of Mullil.

---

* See Sayce, *Hibbert Lectures*, p. 362.

## SHEOL. 155

The grave (Sheol) from beneath is moved for thee, to meet thee at thy coming; it stirreth up the dead (*rephaim*) for thee, even all the chief ones (*alim*); it hath raised up from their thrones all the kings of the nations.
All they shall speak and say unto thee, Art thou become weak as we? Art thou become like unto us?

In this quotation, the grave where the "feeble ones," the ancestral ghosts, the *niši* or spirits, the *anunas* or "masters," sit on their thrones and hail each new-comer with the cry, "Art thou become weak as we?" is almost the exact phraseology of the Babylonian Tablets. Notice here the contrast between the dark region of the grave, Sheol, and the bright summit of the Mountain of Assembly. "For thou hast said in thine heart, I will ascend unto heaven, I will exalt my throne above the stars of God. I will sit upon the Mount of the Congregation in the sides (uttermost parts) of the North. I will ascend above the heights of the clouds, I will be like the Most High."

As yet the conception conveys only the idea of a vast, dark palace of the god of the ghost-world, in which the great dead sit on thrones in silent conclave. However, the conception is still growing and gaining shape. The important inscription quoted indicates this development.

A mythological text, of whatever nature, always gains a vast amount in value when its date can be assigned. Among the Tablets found at Tel el-Amarna\* is one, unfortunately mutilated, describing the grave-land, the under-world. This inscription, and the ideas it conveys, cannot, on historical grounds, be later than B.C. 1400, or about a century before the age of Moses.

---

\* Tel el-Amarna Tablets in the British Museum, pl. 17, text No. 82.

The opening portion of this Tablet, much mutilated, may be read as follows:—

> When the gods had appointed a banquet
> To their sister Eris-kigal
> They sent a messenger.

But she being the wife of the god Nergal, the lord of the under-world, is forbidden to come to the banquet in the "highest heavens" (*samie zirute*). The gods are angry that one of their number should refuse to be present at the feast, and send to fetch her. The ambassador chosen is the god Namtar, "the pestilence god," who is the messenger* between the under-world and heaven. He is here called the "Messenger of Eris-kigal"; and it was he who acted like the Greek Hermes, who led souls from the under-world to heaven. In the above myth there is evidently an early form of the Greek legend of Persephone, and which, if the inscription were complete, would furnish much more interesting matter. It is, however, even in its mutilated form, a document of much importance.

### REVERSE.

> The god Assaku in the second, the god Isum
> In the third, the god Mitbariga in the fourth,
> The god Sabta in the fifth, the god Rabitza in the sixth, Dirid
> In the seventh, Ilutu in the eighth, Binna in the ninth,
> Zidana in the tenth, Mikid in the eleventh, Birnpari
> In the twelfth, Umma in the thirteenth, Liba in the fourteenth.
> In the gateway was standing the god Khuduma, who in the couch cuts off.
> Namtar to his host a command made, the gates.

---

* The *Iukanu*, or messengers of the gods, correspond to the *melek*, or "angel" of the Hebrew Scriptures, as in the narratives of Hagar (Gen. 21. 17) or Balaam (Num. 22. 22). Namtar corresponded to the "Angel of Death."

In the midst of the palace he seized Eris-kigal
By her hair and dragged her from the throne
To the ground, her head to cut off.
" Do not slay me, O my brother! a word may I speak to thee"
Heard Nergal, and lifted his hand he wept . . . . .
"Thou truly art my husband, I truly thy wife. Then take to
thyself
Sovereignty in the wide earth, and establish, good
For power is at thy hand. Then thou shalt be lord
And lady." Nergal gave ear to her words.
He took her and kissed her, her tears, he covered :
"Whatsoever thou askest of me in future for all time it is
done."

We have here a more definite form given to the underworld. It is that of a great city, a vast underground, dark city of the dead, encircled by seven walls, with seven sets of double gates, each guarded by a pair of gods. This was the city of the dead, called *Urugal*, or " the Great City," to which all the dead flocked. It is represented as having its palace and its rulers. The king of the city of the dead was Nergal, or, in its older form, Ner, " the strong one," because, as Death, he conquered all. The name Nergal, which is known as that of the god of the colonists from Kutha, placed in Samaria (2 Kings 18. 30) is probably *Ner-gal*, " the great ruler"; or it may be, as I think, a corruption of " *Ner-uru-gal*," the " ruler of the Great City." The worship of Nergal centred in the city of Kutha, about twenty miles east of Babylon, now marked by the mounds of Tel-Ibrahim. This city was known by the name of Gudua to the Akkadians, of which the Semitic Kutha is a corruption, the name meaning "the resting place." It was also called Tigabba, or the " city of the bowing down of the head," a fit name for the sacred city of the god of Death, and was the chief necropolis of Chaldea.

Among the Semites of Babylonia, and at a later time among the Assyrians, the god of Death became the god of War; and it is as such that Nergal is best known to us. In the Obelisk inscription of Shalmanesar II. (B.C. 860) he is called "Nergal the Valiant, the King of Battles." This phase of the Battle god as the god of Death was largely developed under Assyrian influence. Nergal, as the god of Death, was symbolised by the winged lion, and as such was identified with the god Irkalla, "the Great Eater"—a name which reminds us of the riddle of Samson: "Out of the eater came forth meat; out of the strong came forth sweetness" (Judg. 14. 14). This name evidently refers to the all-devouring character of the god of Death. Another interesting expression of this all-ruling power of death is symbolised by a phrase often found in the hymns of the Early Chaldean Age, "Mankind, the cattle of the god Ner." Just as the king was the shepherd of the nations upon earth, so all mankind had to return home, in the evening of life, to the fold of the god of Death.

In the further development of the eschatology of the Babylonians, the god Nergal loses prominence before his wife, "Eris-kigal," who becomes the queen of the underworld. "Eris-kigal," written in characters Ninkigal, and formerly rendered "The Lady of the Great Land." The Tel el-Amarna Tablet above quoted, however, has given us the correct reading of the name, and at the same time has thrown great light upon the mythology connected with it. The name "Eris-kigal" is to be further rendered as "*Eris-birutu, kigal* being explained in the Assyrian syllabaries by *Birutu*, "pit," the Hebrew בור, "pit, dungeon," a word having an undoubted eschatological meaning in the Hebrew Scriptures, as in

WINGED HUMAN-HEADED LION.
(*Photographed from the original.*)

"the pit of destruction" (Ps. 55. 23), "pit of corruption" (Isa. 38. 17), and many other examples. Eriskigal was the wife of Nergal, but at the same time retained her position as the "sister of the great gods" in heaven, occupying exactly the position of the Greek Persephone. As Queen of Hades she was the rival of the Celestial Venus, and the rivalry is well shown in the beautiful poem known to scholars as the "Tablet of the Descent of Istar into the Under-world," from which the following extracts are taken:—

### THE DESCENT OF ISTAR.

To the land whence none return, the region of darkness,
Istar, daughter of the Moon-God, firmly set her mind,
Even the daughter of the Moon-God fixed her mind (to go)
To the house of darkness, the seat of the great Devourer,
To the house whose entrance has no exit,
By the road whose going has no return,
To the house from whose entrance light is shut out,
The place where much dust is their bread, their food mud;
Light they see not, in darkness they dwell,
Clad also like birds with a robe of feathers:
Over the door and bolt dust is scattered.
Istar on arriving at the gate of the land of No-Return,
To the porter of the gate a word she utters:
"Oh, porter of the waters, open thy gate!
Open thy gate that I may enter!
If thou openest not thy gate that I may enter,
I will smite the doors, the bolt I will break;
I will smite the threshold, tear away the portals,
I will raise the dead, the devourers (*akili*) of the living,
Over the living the dead shall exceed in number."
The porter opens his mouth and speaks;
He says to Istar the princess,
"Stay, O lady, thou must not break it down!

Let me go and declare thy name to Eris-Kigal, the Lady of Hades."

The keeper descended, and declared her name to Eris-Kigal:
" Oh goddess, the waters thy sister Istar is (come to seek),
Trying the mighty bars—(to break open the doors)."
When Allat heard this she opened her mouth and said,
" Like a cut-off reed has she descended,
Like the petal (lip) of a drooping reed she prays for the waters of life:
What brings her heart to me, what brings her mind to me?

\*    \*    \*    \*    \*    \*    \*

Like food would I eat, like sweet drink would I drink;
Let me weep for the heroes who have left their wives;
Let me weep for the handmaids whom from the bosom of their husbands thou hast taken;
For the young child let me weep, whom thou hast taken before his day:
Go, keeper, open for her the gate;
Strip her according to the law of old time."
The first gate he made her enter, and shut it; he threw down the mighty crown of her head.
" Why, O keeper, dost thou throw down the mighty crown of my head."
" Enter, O lady, such are the orders of the Lady of the Land."
The second gate he made her enter, and he shut; he threw away the earrings of her ears.
" Wherefore, O keeper, hast thou thrown away the earrings of my ears?"
" Enter, O lady, for such are the orders of the Lady of the Land."
The third gate he made her to enter, and he closed; he threw away the precious stones of her neck.
" Wherefore, O keeper, hast thou thrown away the precious stones of my neck?"
" Enter, O lady, these are the orders of the Lady of the Land."
The fourth gate he made her enter, and closed; he threw away the ornaments of her breast.

" Wherefore, O keeper, hast thou thrown away the ornaments
   of my breast ? "
" Enter, O lady, such are the orders of the Lady of the Land."
The fifth gate he made her to enter, and closed; he threw
   away the jewelled girdle of her waist.
" Wherefore, O keeper, hast thou taken away the jewelled
   girdle of my waist ? "
" Enter, O lady, such are the orders of the Lady of the Land."
The sixth gate he made her enter, and closed; he threw away
   the circlets of her hands and feet.
" Wherefore, O keeper, hast thou thrown away the circlets of
   my hands and feet ? "
" Enter, O lady, such are the orders of the Lady of the Land."
The seventh gate he made her enter, and closed ; he threw away
   the robe of her body.
" Wherefore, O keeper, hast thou thrown away the robe of my
   body ? "
" Enter, O lady, such are the orders of the Lady of the Land."
So soon as Istar had descended into the " Land of No-Return,"
Eris-Kigal beheld her, and was enraged toward her—
Istar took no thought,—she cried to her with oaths,
Eris-Kigal opened her mouth and said,
To Namtar, her messenger, the word she utters:
" Go, Namtar, (take Istar from) me and
Lead her out ; sixty times afflict her :
The disease of the eyes into her eyes;
The disease of the side into her side ;
The disease of the feet into her feet ;
The disease of heart into her heart ;
The disease of the head afflict her head ;
Into her, even the whole of her, strike disease."

There are some passages of difficulty, and as they have no great bearing on the subject of the chapter they are omitted. From these lines it appears that during the absence of the goddess there was no love on earth, and no increase of flock or herd, and so the gods decided to restore the lost one. The task is assigned to the all-wise god Ea.

Ea in the wisdom of his heart formed a creature,
He created Azu-su-namir the androgne.
" Go, Azu-su-namir, towards the gate of Hades set thy face ;
Let the seven gates of Hades be opened before thee ;
Let the Lady of the Land see thee and rejoice at thy presence,
When her heart is at rest and her liver appeased.
Conjure her also by the names of the great gods';
Turn thy head ; to the resting-place of the cold wind set
 thy mind,
The home of the pure one, in the resting-place of the cold wind ;
Let them prepare the waters in the midst, let her drink."
When the lady of the land heard this
She tore her girdle, she bit her thumb :
" Thou hast asked of me a request none should ask.
Go, Azu-su-namir, let me injure thee with a great injury :
May the garbage of the sewers of the city be thy food !
May the vessels of the daughters of the city be thy drink ;
May the darkness of the dungeon be thy habitation ;
May the threshold be thy seat ;
May drought and famine strike thy offspring."
The Lady of the Land opened her mouth and said,
To Namtar, her messenger, a word she addresses :
" Go, Namtar, strike the firmly-built palace,
Shatter the thresholds which hide the stones of light ;
Bid the Anunas come forth and seat them on the throne of gold ;
Over Istar pour the waters of life and bring her before me."

The goddess is now released, and as she returns through each of the seven gates her articles of adornment are restored to her. Then follows some lines of special interest to the Biblical student, describing the release of the lover of the goddess, Tammuz or Adonis, to rescue whom she had gone into the dread land.

" If she has not given thee that for which the ransom is paid,
 turn back to her again
For Tammuz, the bridegroom of thy youth :
Pour over him the pure waters, anoint him with holy oil ;

Clothe him with a purple robe, a ring of lapis lazuli let him
    put on his hand.
Let Samkhat (the goddess of pleasure) rest the mind.
The goddess Tillili take her jewels,
The onyx stones which are unbroken.
The goddess Tillili had heard of the carrying below of
    her brother;
She broke her jewels,
Even the onyx stones which were full of light,
Crying, ' Oh, my brother, the only one, do not leave me.'
In the day that Tammuz bound me with a ring of crystal
    and a circlet of turquoise. . . .
Let the waiting-men and waiting-women surround the funeral
    pyre and smell the sweet savour."

There is, perhaps, no text in the whole range of Assyriological literature which contains so much matter of interest alike for the student of Classical Mythology and of the Bible as this inscription.

## The Weeping for Tammuz.

The legend of the descent of Istar is in reality a species of miracle play, which was part of the liturgy of the great festival of the mourning for the dead Tammuz, so universal throughout the East.

Although not of Semitic origin, the worship of the youthful Sun-god Tammuz seems to have been adopted readily by Phœnicians, Syrians, Hebrews, and the people of Asia Minor, as well as the Greeks. The text throws much light upon this cultus.

In the Scripture the most definite reference to it is found in the Book of Ezekiel (8. 14): "Then he brought me to the door of the gate of the LORD'S house, which was towards the North, and, behold, there sat women weeping for

Tammuz." Upon this passage we have much illustrative matter. The Son of Life (Dumzi), or Tammuz, the youthful summer sun, was slain by the "boar's tusk," that is, by the cold blast of the north winds of winter, and, therefore, it is towards the North that the Hebrew women were weeping. So also in the Tablet the rescuer of Istar and Tammuz is directed to "turn thy heads to the resting place of the cold wind; set thy mind toward the resting place of the cold wind." The North was regarded as an evil death-dealing quarter, for thence came the wind *Iltanu* or *Istanū*, from *Satanu*, "hostile evil." The mountain of the north and north-east, the mountain of the World, in whose interior was the land of Aralli, the house of dearth, situated in the evil North.

A most pointed reference to this mourning is found in the prophecy of Jeremiah, regarding the death of Jehoiakim the son of Josiah, where he quotes in derision of the wicked king the funeral dirge of Tammuz: "They shall not lament for him, Ah, my brother! or, Ah, sister! They shall not lament for him, saying, Ah, lord, or, Ah, his glory" (Jer. 22. 18), where we have almost the words of the Tablet, "Oh, my brother, the only one." It is probably to a similar mourning that the prophet Zechariah refers (12. 11) "in the mourning for Hadad-Rimmon."

In Phœnicia the festivals of Tammuz were observed with great ceremonial in the glen of Apacha (weeping). This beautiful glen, about eight miles north of Beyrout, is the source of the Adonis river—the modern "Nahr Ibrahim." The rains of the spring and the melting snows of Lebanon combined to redden the waters of the stream with the red marl of the mountains, in which the priests of Gebal, with poetic fancy, saw the blood of the slain Sun-god, and in the

## SHADOW OF DEATH. 165

month of Tammuz (June—July) there was held here the festival of the god.

At a later period, when Babylonian and Assyrian influence on the priesthood of Phœnicia was replaced by that of Egypt, the god Tammuz became identified with Osiris, and Istar with Isis, and the ceremonial became more complicated.

In Tammuz, in this legend, as in Osiris in the Egyptian "Book of the Dead," we see the type of the deceased, and thus learn more of the theory of future life held by the ancient Babylonians. In each legend the hero is the sun, dying and rising again to life in its original sphere of existence.

### THE LAND OF DARKNESS AND DEATH.

The description given in the tablet is most vivid. It is that of a great city (*uru gal*) with its walls and gates and with the outer wall circled by "the waters" of the river of death. This city of the dead was called by the Babylonians by the name of *Sualu*—the exact equivalent of the Hebrew Sheol.* The lexigraphical tablet in which this important word is found throws considerable light on the meaning. In the list of words from which the name is taken, the majority are derivatives of the root *Ḳabaru*, the Hebrew קָבַר, *Ḳabur*, "to bury," and *Ḳebir*, "a grave," and *Sualu* is an equivalent of *Alu Ḳabru*, "city of the grave." We have seen already that another name was *Kigal* or *birutu*, "the pit," so that both the usual Hebrew renderings of Sheol—the grave and the pit—are also to be found in the inscriptions. Another name of the

---

* See Delitzsch, *Hebrew and Assyrian*, p. 26.

region of death was that of *Bit Muti,* "the house of death," or Aralli; while in the Tablet under consideration it is also called *mat la tairat,* "the Land of No-Return," which is especially the land of darkness. In the inscription this is most clearly stated, and in almost the very words of Scripture; "the Land of No-Return, the region of darkness;" "the house of darkness;" "the house at whose entrance they shut out the light;" "light they see not, in darkness they dwell." With these compare such passages as "He shall go to the generation of his fathers;[*] they shall never see light" (Ps. 49. 16). In the Book of Job, which is so full of valuable passages regarding the future state, there are many references to this land of darkness: "Let darkness and the shadow of death claim it for their own" (3. 5); "He bringeth out to light the shadow of death" (12. 22). Mark also the contrast in the words "He hath redeemed my soul from going into the pit, and my life shall behold the light" (Job 33. 18). So also "Declare, if thou knowest at all, where is the way of the dwelling of light; and, as for darkness, where is the place thereof" (Job 38. 19). These passages show that to the Hebrew, as to the Babylonian, darkness was associated with the Land of No-Return, and the house of death.

THE SHADOW OF DEATH.

There is a phrase in the Scriptures very frequently associated with Sheol, which is also found in the Babylonian religious inscriptions. This is the "Shadow of Death," *Zalmoth,* צַלְמָוֶת, which has its exact equivalent in the Hebrew *Zalmat.* In one of the last of the books of

---

[*] A curious resemblance to the Anunas or Masters of the Babylonian "ghost land."

the Chaldean Epic of Gilgames—the book of darkness as we may call it—we have a very important passage : " O, darkness (*Zalmat*) ! O, darkness, Mother of many waters ; O, darkness, her mighty power as a garment covers thee." In the same inscription, unfortunately very fragmentary, also occurs a passage of great value. The hero Gilgames, afraid of death, asks what manner of place the grave is, and receives as his reply, " It is the place thou comest to when thou growest old and the worm enters, and thou hast put on corruption." With which we may compare the words in Job, " If I have said to corruption, Thou art my father : to the worm, Thou art my mother and my sister " (**17. 14**) ; and again also, " they lie alike in the dust, and the worm covereth them " (**21. 26**).

It is evident that in this later teaching, as to the grave-land, it was believed to be below the earth, and reached as it were by a yawning pit. A fragmentary tablet in the British Museum reads : " To the Land of No-Return I turn myself, I spread like a bird my hands ; I descend, I descend to the house of darkness, the dwelling of the great devourer." The same conception is also common to the Hebrew writings, as in the case of Korah, Dathan, and Abiram in Num. **16**. 30, or as implied in the words of Isaiah (**14. 9**) : " Sheol from *beneath* is moved for thee." Indeed, the idea of a yawning bottomless pit, which some consider to be implied by the word Sheol, seems to be borne out by the passage in Job, "What is deeper than Sheol ? " (**11. 8**).

I now pass to a much more important and, at the same time, more difficult phase of the subject, namely, the consideration of the question, Was the Hades of the Babylonians regarded as a place of punishment ? This is a very difficult question to answer; sources of evidence being as yet far from complete. From the tablet of the descent of Istar it would certainly seem to be so.

The goddess, who, as already stated, represents the deceased, is stripped naked and bare, and instead of her ornaments is clothed with disease. In the same manner the creature Aza-su-namir undergoes vicatory punishment for her. "Let me injure thee with a great injury; may the garbage of the sewers of the city be thy food; may the darkness of the dungeon be thy habitation," certainly seem to imply punishment.

In the same manner the words of Istar herself seem to indicate that she knew the circle of the under-world to which she would be assigned.

" Let me weep for the heroes who have left their wives; let me weep for the handmaids who from the bosoms of their husbands have turned; let me weep for the little child whom thou hast taken ere his days are come." It was to the cycle described in the Talmudic writers of faithless wives, husbands, and adulterers, and those who had procured abortion that the goddess, who had ruined " families through her witchcrafts " (Nah. 3. 4), was to be assigned.[*]

There seems to have been also a species of judgment, as the frequent reference to the *rules* and "ancient laws" imply.

There was, however, no approach to the elaborate tribunal of the forty-two assessors of the Egyptian "Book of the Dead."

In the Egyptian ritual the deceased was judged by Osiris and his forty-two assessors, his heart being placed on one

---

[*] See the interesting details regarding this cycle in the recently discovered *Apocalypse of St. Peter*.

side of the scale held by Horus and Anubis,* while the scribe Thoth registered the result of the weighing. Upon this, judgment was given in the Hall of "the Two Truths," and the fate of the deceased was decided. In the 124th chapter of the Book of the Dead,† called the chapter of the going to the Hall of the Two Truths, and of the separating of a person from his sins, when he had been made to see the faces of the gods, the whole ceremonial is set forth. The worst form of punishment was that of annihilation and destruction by the hippopotamus-shaped Devourer.

After passing through the various trials and troubles the soul, according to Egyptian teaching, entered the abode of beatified spirits, and remained in bliss until it rejoined the body in the tomb.

As the Egyptian creed did not imply a resurrection to immortal life in heaven, so there does not seem any real trace of such a belief in the teaching of Babylonia. Merodach, as I have already said, could raise the dead to life; but it was only a restoration to life here, not to eternal life in heaven with God.

Immortality could only be obtained by drinking of the "waters of life" which rose in the mystic fountain in the centre of the palace of the under-world, and were guarded by the Anunas. Istar only obtained her release when Namtar "had poured out for her the waters of life."

With the gradual predominance of Semitic thought there arose another belief in the attainment of immortality. This was by leading the perfect life which led to translation or deification. Just as "Enoch was a just man and walked

---
* Jackal-headed god. See illustration, p. 134.
† In this chapter occurs the famous "Negative confession," which by some is regarded as the source of the Decalogue.

with God, and God took him" (Gen. 5. 24), so Elijah, in whom was a perfect manifestation of the prophetic life, ascended to heaven, so Samas-Napisti, the Chaldean Noah, "who only had been the servant of the gods," was translated or deified, or absorbed into the gods. This same idea is well expressed by the words in the Deluge Tablet: "Formerly Samas-Napisti was as mankind (*amilutum-ma*). From now Samas-Napisti and his wife, to be like gods, are borne away, and there to dwell Samas-Napisti at the mouth of the river in a remote place they took us. And in a remote place at the mouth of the rivers they caused us to dwell."

### The Conception of Heaven.

It is one of the most fascinating and, at the same time, one of the most difficult subjects in the study of the mythological literature of an ancient people to ascertain the conception which they formed of the future state of the blessed.

It may be generally assumed that the conception of heaven which an ancient people form, is usually an idealised, beatified form of the happiest life on earth. The North-American Indian has his "happy hunting grounds"; the Norseman his "Valhalla," with its perpetual wassail and banquet with golden cups of mead; and the Mohammedan his "paradise" of harem delights; while the peaceful ancient Egyptian had his "happy fields."

It is also to be noticed that as a nation rises in the scale of civilisation so the conception of heaven becomes grander and brighter. The heaven of a wandering people, living in tents and rich in flocks and herds, differs from that of a city-dwelling people whose greatness centres in a court or king, and where the law that might is right holds sway. The one is the eternal fields, the other sees before him the court or camp, the place of mighty warriors.

In Babylonian and Assyrian literature we have these several stages of development represented by texts of various ages.

The earliest conception of heaven is a simple one, set forth in one of the hymns of the primitive Chaldean age.

The text is one of the litanies of the religio-magical creed, and relates to the healing of a sick man:—

"On the butter which is brought from a pure stall,
The milk which is brought from a pure sheepcote,
The pure butter of the pure stall, lay a spell.
May the' man, the son of his god, recover;
May the man be bright and pure as the butter,
May he be white as this milk."

Here is the heaven of the shepherd, with the blessed flocks and herds. References to a place of happiness and a heaven are very scarce, indeed almost wanting in the older Akkadian pre-Semitic literature of Babylonia. It is true they had the "sky-god Ana," and the "Spirit of heaven" is invoked in the magical litanies, but it is certainly rather the natural all-covering sky than the abode of the risen blessed.

With the advent of the Semites the conception is changed and extended. Anna under the form of Anu becomes no longer the god of the visible vault of heaven, but the king of the invisible world above the all-covering sky, the serene and happy regions above the clouds, where the gods held court. It is the land of the "silver sky," the heaven of Anu, the seventh heaven, to which the gods ascended when the terrible Deluge took place, and where the court of the Sky-god has replaced the summit of the World Mountain.

## THE HEAVEN OF ANU.

Just as we were fortunate in having recovered an inscription (of which we could ascertain the approximate date) describing the under-world, so from the same source we have obtained one which contains a description of heaven. Among the tablets from Tel el-Amarna in Egypt which formed part of the library of the heretic Pharaoh, Amenophis IV. (Khu-en Aten), who reigned about B.C. 1430, is one containing the legend of a certain Adapa, the fisherman of the god Ea, who was permitted to enter heaven to obtain pardon from the god Anu for having broken the wings of the south wind. The tablet is unfortunately broken both at the beginning and end. Adapa, man of the god Ea, was fishing in the midst of the sea, in the house of the fishes, to catch fish for his master Ea. The sea was smooth, but the south wind blew and caused the sea to sweep over Adapa and to sink him in the sea. In his rage he threatens to break the wings of the south wind. The text now becomes more complete :—

> As he spoke thus with his mouth, the wings of the south wind were broken.
> For seven days the south wind blew no more across the land.
> Then Anu spake thus to his messenger the god Ilabrat.
> "Why has the south wind not blown across the land these seven days?"
> His messenger, the god Ilabrat, answered him, "My lord, Adapa, the son of the god Ea, hath broken the wings of the south wind."
> When Anu heard these words he cried out "Help!"

The next few lines are too mutilated for consecutive translation. They describe how Anu orders Adapa to be brought before him, and how Ea arrays his son in a shroud and warns him as to his conduct when going before the god of heaven. "When thou risest up to heaven and reachest the gate of Anu, the god Tammuz and the god Giz-zida (Tree of Life) will stand at the gate of Anu; they will see thee, and call out 'Help, help, Lord! For whom dost thou mourn, O Adapa? For whom hast thou put on a shroud?' 'Two gods have died in our land' (shalt thou answer), 'therefore do I this.' 'Who are the two gods that have died in thy land?' Then shall the god Tammuz and the god Giz-zida look upon each other and raise their voices in lamentation. Then shall they speak a word of favour before Anu, and cause thee to behold the beautiful face of Anu."

> "When thou comest in to the presence of Anu they will offer thee food of death. Eat it not.
> Water of death they will offer thee. Drink it not.
> A garment they will offer thee. Put it on.
> Oil they will offer thee. Anoint thyself with it.
> Despise not the words I have given thee; ponder upon the words I have spoken to thee."
> Then the messenger of Anu arrived, "Adapa has broken the wings of the south wind." "Bring him before me" (said Anu).

Here there is again a break in the tablet, and when we can resume, it reads:—"When he had risen up to the gate of heaven, and had reached the gate of Anu, the god Tammuz and the god Giz-zida stood at the gate of Anu. When they saw Adapa they called out 'Help, Lord! For whom dost thou mourn, Adapa? For whom hast thou put on a shroud?' 'Two gods have died in our land, therefore do I put on a shroud.' 'Who are the two gods that have died in the land?' The god Tammuz and the god Giz-zida looked at each other and raised their voices in lamentation. When Adapa now drew near to the presence of Anu, Anu saw him, and said, 'O Adapa, why hast thou broken the wings of the south wind?' And Adapa answered Anu, 'My lord, in the midst of the sea I was catching fish for the house of my lord, while still and smooth lay the waters around me. Then rose the south wind and dipped me into the waters.'" Then follow some more fragmentary lines in which Adapa relates how, in the anger of his heart, he broke the wings of the south wind. Then the god Tammuz and the god Giz-zida spoke a favourable word to the god Anu, and he answered, "Why did Anu permit a sinful man to behold the innermost parts of heaven and earth. He made him great and gave him renown; but what shall we grant him? Let food of life be offered him, so that he may eat."*

"Then food of life was offered him and he ate not. Water of life was offered him and he drank not. A garment was offered to him and he clothed himself. Oil was offered to him and he anointed himself. Then Anu looked upon him and raised his voice in lamentation, O Adapa, wherefore eatest thou not? Wherefore drinkest thou not? The gift of life cannot be thine. I remembered the words of Ea, my lord which he spake to me: Eat not, drink not, but put on the garment and anoint thyself; and Anu let him return to his own land." Con-

---

* I am indebted to the rendering of this list to the Transactions of the Ninth International Congress of Orientalists, London, by Prof. Sayce, for the reading of many obscure passages.

fused as this text is, due in some measure, I think, to its being a student's copy, it contains some matter of interest. The entrance to heaven can only be through death, and therefore Adapa disguises himself as one dead by wearing a shroud, and immortality is only gained by eating the "food of (eternal) life, and drinking the waters of (eternal) life," which are the food and waters of death to mortals. Of special interest is the mention of the robe with which the inhabitants of heaven are clothed. In another text in the British Museum this is called the "robe of brightness," reminding us of the "wedding garment" in the parable (Matt. 22. 11). The anointing with oil also forms a curious parallel to the "oil of gladness" (Ps. 45. 7).

The position of Tammuz and Giz-zida reminds us, as Professor Sayce has pointed out, of the pillars Jachin and Boaz at the gates of the Temple (1 Kings 7. 21). It is also curious to find the god of the Tree of Life forming the guardians of the gate of heaven, for after the Fall, man was shut out from eating of the tree, "lest he put forth his hand and take also of the Tree of Life, and eat, and live for ever" (Gen. 3. 22).

There are other inscriptions which show that the Assyrians had a clear idea of a place of happiness to which those who had "eaten the food of life or drank the waters of life" would go to dwell.

In a hymn of the late age of Assurbanipal (B.C. 668) there is a passage which indicates this belief: "As a man may he live and be at peace. Over kings and princes may he exercise wide-spread dominion. May he come to grey hairs. For the men who utter these prayers may the land of the silver sky, oil unceasing, and wine of blessedness be their food, and a perpetual noon-day their light. Health to thy body and prosperity is my prayer to the gods who dwell in the land of Assyria."

We cannot compare these passages with any in the Old Testament, for it is remarkable to note how lacking these books are in any description of the future abode of the blessed; indeed, only one text can be quoted with any certainty. "Thou wilt show me the path of life, in thy presence is fulness of joy; at thy right hand there are pleasures for evermore" (Ps. 16. 11).

It was not until the advent of Christianity, with its wider hopes, with its grand doctrine of the resurrection and the Kingdom of Heaven, that the true conception of the life of heaven was realized.

A true conception of the nature of sin, and of the alienation thereby from God, enlarged and spiritualised the crude material conceptions of Judaism, and out of them came the beautiful conceptions of the Kingdom of Heaven which adorn the New Testament.

Symbols already familiar to us appear in Assyrian and Babylonian mythology, such as the "Marriage Feast," the "River of Life," the "Throne of God," and other conceptions, but all have a new and truer meaning in the teaching of Christ.

There can be little doubt that during the period of the later Babylonian Empire, from B.C. 606–538, and during the Persian rule, the teaching of the Babylonian priests underwent many changes and attained to a higher and purer form. It was during these and subsequent ages that much of the eschatology which we find in Jewish and apocalyptic writers grew up, and that the Kingdom of Heaven began to assume a definite shape in the religious teachings of the age, but no definite conclusion can as yet be arrived at owing to the dearth at present of religious texts of this period. That throughout long ages the Babylonians had been developing a definite scheme of belief as to the future life is perfectly evident from the testimony of the Monuments.

# HER MAJESTY'S PRINTERS'
## Special Publications.

---

THE STUDENT'S HANDBOOK TO THE PSALMS.

LEX MOSAICA; OR, THE OLD TESTAMENT AND THE HIGHER CRITICISM.

THE BIBLE STUDENT'S LIBRARY.

SPECIAL EDITIONS OF THE HOLY BIBLE.

SPECIAL EDITIONS OF THE BOOK OF COMMON PRAYER.

&c. &c.

## EYRE & SPOTTISWOODE,
### Her Majesty's Printers:
LONDON—GREAT NEW STREET, FLEET STREET, E.C.
EDINBURGH, GLASGOW, MELBOURNE, SYDNEY, AND NEW YORK.

### Government Publications Sale Office:
EAST HARDING STREET, LONDON, E.C.

# CONTENTS.

| | PAGE |
|---|---|
| THE STUDENT'S HANDBOOK TO THE PSALMS | 3 |
| LEX MOSAICA; OR, THE OLD TESTAMENT, AND THE HIGHER CRITICISM | 4 |
| THE QUEEN'S PRINTERS' Bible Student's Library:— | |
|    VOL. I. THE FOUNDATIONS OF THE BIBLE | 6 |
|    VOL. II. THE LAW IN THE PROPHETS | 7 |
|    VOL. III. THE PRINCIPLES OF BIBLICAL CRITICISM | 8 |
| THE QUEEN'S PRINTERS' Special Editions of the Holy Bible:— | |
|    THE VARIORUM REFERENCE BIBLE (Large Type) | 9 |
|    THE VARIORUM REFERENCE APOCRYPHA (Large Type) | 10 |
|    THE VARIORUM REFERENCE TEACHER'S BIBLE (Large Type) | 12 |
|    THE VARIORUM REFERENCE TEACHER'S BIBLE (Nonpareil 8vo.) | 12 |
| THE QUEEN'S PRINTERS' TEACHER'S BIBLE (New Edition, 1894) | 14 |
|    AIDS TO BIBLE STUDENTS (New Edition, 1894) | 15, 16 |
|    THE MARKED LECTERN BIBLE (*in red and black*) | 21 |
|    THE FAMILY BIBLE WITH COMMENTARY | 22 |
| THE QUEEN'S PRINTERS' Special Editions of the Book of Common Prayer:— | |
|    THE ANNEXED BOOK OF 1662 IN TYPE (*with Appendices*) | 23 |
|    THE HISTORICAL PRAYER BOOK | 23 |
|    BARRY'S TEACHER'S PRAYER BOOK (*with Glossary*) | 24 |
| SELECT GLOSSARY OF BIBLE WORDS, ALSO A GLOSSARY OF IMPORTANT WORDS AND PHRASES IN THE PRAYER BOOK | 25 |
| THE PSALTER WITH COMMENTARY (Large Type) | 25 |
| HYMNS FOR CHILDREN AND CHILDREN'S PRAYERS (Illustrated) | 26 |
| THE IMITATION OF CHRIST, CHRISTIAN YEAR, &c. | 26 |
| THE RHYTHM OF S. BERNARD (Illustrated) | 26 |
| OLD BIBLES: AN ACCOUNT OF THE VARIOUS VERSIONS OF THE ENGLISH BIBLE | 26 |
| THE BATTLE OF THE STANDPOINTS | 26 |

## THE
# STUDENT'S HANDBOOK TO THE PSALMS.

BY THE

### Rev. J. SHARPE, D.D.,
*Late Fellow of Christ College, Cambridge.*

Size, small 4to., cloth, bevelled boards, gilt top, price 12/-

THIS Handbook aims at treating the poetry and theology of the Psalms in such a manner as shall benefit not only the student of the Hebrew, but also the English reader who takes an intelligent interest in the controversies of the day, and finds in the Psalms the daily food of devotion.

The work will be of use to students for theological degrees, and to all who adopt the purpose of St. Paul: "*I will sing with the spirit and I will sing with the understanding also.*"—1 Cor. 14. 15.

### SOME OPINIONS OF THE PRESS.

**The Times.**—"Very useful to students and devout readers."

**Literary World.**—"Dr. Sharpe has taken infinite pains to place his subject as clearly as possible before the English reader."

**Record.**—"Dr. Sharpe is to be warmly thanked for his book. It is good to find a scholar referring to the 'old paths' and confessing that 'continued study ever demonstrates more fully' their superiority."

**The Christian World.**—"It is full of useful information."

**Sunday School Chronicle.**—"The book is one which Sunday School Teachers will find exceptionally useful."

**The Irish Times.**—"This handbook to the Psalms will be invaluable to every earnest Christian student. Dr. Sharpe lays the Christian communities under an obligation everywhere."

**The Scotsman.**—"The book will be highly prized by those who 'stand in the old paths' and which those who are seeking to advance will find worthy of their considerations."

**Western Morning News.**—"A scholarly and valuable book, which should be found in all theological libraries."

### RETAIL OF ALL BOOKSELLERS.

*EYRE & SPOTTISWOODE.*

# LEX MOSAICA;

OR,

*THE LAW OF MOSES AND THE HIGHER CRITICISM.*

EDITED BY THE

Rev. RICHARD VALPY FRENCH, D.C.L., LL.D., F.S.A.,

WITH AN INTRODUCTION BY THE LATE

RIGHT REVEREND LORD ARTHUR C. HERVEY, D.D.,

*Bishop of Bath and Wells.*

Essays by Various Writers on the Law of Moses and the Higher Criticism.

LIST OF CONTRIBUTORS:

Rev. A. H. SAYCE, D.D., LL.D.
Rev. GEORGE RAWLINSON, M.A.
Rev. GEORGE C. M. DOUGLAS, D.D.
Rev. R. B. GIRDLESTONE, M.A.
Rev. RICHARD VALPY FRENCH, D.C.L., LL.D., F.S.A.
Rev. J. J. LIAS, M.A.
Rev. F. WATSON, D.D.

Rev. J. SHARPE, D.D.
Rev. ALEXANDER STEWART, LL.D., F.A.S.
Rev. STANLEY LEATHES, D.D.
Rev. ROBERT SINKER, D.D.
Rev. F. E. SPENCER, M.A.
Rev. ROBERT WATTS, D.D., LL.D.

WITH A SUMMARY BY THE

Rev. HENRY WACE, D.D., Principal of King's College, London.

*Royal 8vo., Half-bound Vellum Cloth, Red Burnished Edges,* **15/-**

RETAIL OF ALL BOOKSELLERS.

*EYRE & SPOTTISWOODE,*

Special Publications. 5

## LEX MOSAICA—*continued.*

## Some Opinions of the Press.

**The Times.**—"A volume of conservative but scholarly Biblical criticism."

**Church Times.**—"Here stands the deliverance of fourteen able men speaking at their best."

**Record.**—"We fully believe that this book will be of great use in this time of unrest."

**Churchman.**—"'Lex Mosaica' is a valuable handbook of this momentous controversy."

**The Tablet.**—"An important contribution to the literature of the subject."

**Expository Times.**—"The most serious effort that has yet been made to stem the advancing tide of Old Testament criticism."

**Church Family Newspaper.**—"The volume is one of great interest, which must command the earnest attention both of Biblical Students and critics."

**Christian.**—"An armoury of facts and arguments against one of the most formidable adversaries of a firm and settled faith in the inspired Word of God."

**Sunday School Chronicle.**—"We very gladly welcome this book. It presents a mass of clear and precise information of priceless value to the Bible students."

**The Methodist Times.**—"The writers of 'Lex Mosaica' deserve the grateful thanks of all who believe in the Old Testament as a revelation of God, given through men who were guided in all their work by the operation of the Divine Spirit."

**Christian News.**—"We commend this stately volume to our readers."

**Oxford Journal.**—"The list of contributors to this work is a sufficient guarantee of the thoroughness of the historical investigations contained in it."

**Cambridge Chronicle.**—"'Lex Mosaica' is one of the most elaborate expositions of the historical part of the Bible that has ever been produced."

**Irish Times.**—"The volume of the year."

**Scotsman.**—"An honest, and earnest, and altogether worthy contribution to the literature of a great and important subject."

**Glasgow Herald.**—"It is impossible not to admire the splendid controversial skill which the writers display, and the vigour with which they deal their blows."

**Liverpool Mercury.**—"It is impossible to speak too highly of the learning, research, and dialectical power which mark this volume."

**Bristol Times.**—"The book is at once a brave challenge and a dignified rebuke."

**Yorkshire Post.**—"Another and weighty contribution to the vexed subject of Old Testament criticism."

**Western Morning News.**—"Readers will be surprised at the force which the argument acquires when viewed in the light of the vast array of facts marshalled in these pages."

**Western Mail.**—"It is doubtless the most important contribution to Biblical literature that has appeared for many years in this country."

*GREAT NEW STREET, LONDON, E.C.*

## THE BIBLE STUDENT'S LIBRARY.
Cloth Boards, Red Edges. Demy 8vo. Price 3s. 6d.

*Volumes I.-III. Others in preparation.*

FOURTH EDITION, REVISED.

Volume I.

# THE FOUNDATIONS OF THE BIBLE:
### STUDIES IN OLD TESTAMENT CRITICISM.

BY

## R. B. GIRDLESTONE, M.A.,
*Hon. Canon of Christ Church; late Principal of Wycliffe Hall, Oxford.*

SOME OPINIONS.

**Guardian.**—" Written in a reverent spirit."

**Theological Monthly.**—" Any one who takes up the book will be led, we think, to peruse and ponder till he arrives at a sound conclusion on what is, and must remain, one of the most important matters within human ken."

**Church Review.**—" An invaluable work."

**Rock.**—" Canon Girdlestone as an expert gives us the results of his own personal research. We are taken into the very workshop and shown the methods and processes by which the final results have been attained."

**Churchman.**—" It is worthy to become a text-book in a theological assembly."

**Christian.**—" Will assist many to gain a firm foothold with regard to the verity of Holy Writ."

**Literary Churchman.**—" This is a book of exceeding breadth of learning, and quite exceptional value. We desire to give an unusually emphatic recommendation to this valuable treatise."

**Literary Opinion.**—" The style throughout is clear, elevated, and forcible."

**Globe.**—" A mine of strength to the holders of the ancient faith."

**Quiver.**—" We can heartily commend it."

**Baptist.**—" Canon Girdlestone's arguments will command general respect."

**National Church.**—" This is precisely the kind of work wanted in these critical times."

**Evening News.**—" A perfect armoury of argument and scholarship."

**Yorkshire Post.**—" Shows results as interesting as they are valuable."

**Church Bells.**—" The various topics involved are put in a very interesting way."

**British Weekly.**—" It has a calm and dignified style—beauty itself, with a splendid courtesy to opponents, and altogether it is a pleasant book to read."

RETAIL OF ALL BOOKSELLERS.

*EYRE & SPOTTISWOODE,*

## THE BIBLE STUDENT'S LIBRARY—*continued.*

### Volume II.
# THE LAW IN THE PROPHETS.
BY THE
## REV. STANLEY LEATHES, D.D.,
*Professor of Hebrew, King's College, London; Prebendary of St. Paul's;
Author of " The Structure of the Old Testament";
" The Religion of the Christ" (Bampton Lecture); " Christ and the Bible," &c., &c*

### EXTRACT FROM THE PREFACE.

The late Dr. LIDDON wrote: " How I wish you could see your " way to writing a book on, say, 'The Law and the Prophets,' " putting the Law back into the chronological and authoritative " place from which the new criticism would depose it, and so " incidentally reasserting in the main, and with the necessary " reservations, the Mosaic authorship of the Pentateuch."

This book is partly the result of that suggestion.

### SOME OPINIONS.

**Church Quarterly Review.**—" A careful work."

**Guardian.**—" Deserves wide circulation..... It was an excellent idea thus to collect these allusions."

**Church Times.**—" Most valuable."

**Spectator.**—" Proves the antiquity of the Mosaic Law, by the references that are made to it in the books of the Prophets, books that are conceded on all hands to have at least a considerable relative antiquity. The contention of the extremists, that the whole legal ritual is post-exilian, certainly lays itself open to hostile criticism. The appeal of the Prophets to the Hebrew people seems founded on the fact that there was a covenant which the people had broken."

**Church Review.**—" If Dr. Stanley Leathes had never done any other good thing than he has done in writing this most valuable book, he would be fairly entitled to rank as one of the most successful defenders of Holy Scriptures of our day."

**Baptist Magazine.**—" Dr. Leathes has set an example which all who are opposed to the method and result of modern Biblical criticism would do well to follow. He brings the question to a sound and religious test."

RETAIL OF ALL BOOKSELLERS.

*GREAT NEW STREET, LONDON, E.C.*

## THE BIBLE STUDENT'S LIBRARY—*continued.*

### Volume III.
# PRINCIPLES OF BIBLICAL CRITICISM.

BY THE

### REV. J. J. LIAS, M.A.,

*Rector of East Bergholt; formerly Hulsean Lecturer, and Preacher at the Chapel Royal, Whitehall.*

THE object of this volume is to place before the reader the principles on which the criticism of the Bible has been carried on, as well as the results which are supposed to have been obtained, and to inquire how far those results may be believed to have been successful.

The Author, feeling that the present-day life is far too busy to admit of the perusal of large works filled with a mass of detail, and that the great want in many departments of science—and more especially in theological science—is manuals which shall deal with first principles, has endeavoured to collect the main outlines of the subject, and present it in convenient form, and also to make the facts and arguments set forth intelligible to those whose acquaintance with the learned languages is slender.

### SOME OPINIONS OF THE PRESS.

**The Church Times.**—"We have seldom seen in so small a compass so admirable, and withal temperate, exposition of the ingenious puzzles which German criticism has been weaving under the guise of truth. We gratefully recognize the value and importance of this volume; and a reverent investigation carried on, on the lines here suggested, cannot fail to be profitable to the Biblical student."

**The Record.**—"The book is one that we can very cordially recommend."

**Church Quarterly Review.**—"Mr. Lias is entitled to the gratitude of churchmen."

**Expository Times.**—"Exceedingly useful as a storehouse of facts."

**Spectator.**—"Perhaps the most important chapter is that of 'The Evidence of the Psalms.' Mr. Lias knows that the controversy turns largely on the date of these."

### RETAIL OF ALL BOOKSELLERS.

*EYRE & SPOTTISWOODE,*

## THE NEW BIBLE FOR PREACHERS, TEACHERS, & STUDENTS.

# Large Type VARIORUM Reference Bible,

(*Size,* 9¾ × 6¼ × 1¼ *inches.* 1308 *pages.*)

## WITH APOCRYPHA.

(*Size,* 9¼ × 6¼ × 1¼ *inches.* 276 *pages.*)

### For the TEACHER'S EDITION (1980 pages) see page 12.

The Year 1893 will be remembered by Bible Readers for the Publication of NEW Editions of the various TEACHER'S BIBLES, but most particularly for the

#### Completion of the New Edition of the Variorum Reference Bible.

The **VARIORUM** Edition of the Authorised Version has a great and independent value, whether for daily use or as a standard work of Reference. It meets the wants of every grade of student, from the intelligent reader to the learned reviser.

In its style and appearance the **VARIORUM REFERENCE BIBLE** has been studiously assimilated to the ordinary 8vo. Reference Bible to make its utility no less universal.

This Edition is distinguished from all other Reference Bibles by the addition, *on the same page as the Text*, in Foot-notes, of a complete digest of the chief of the various Renderings and Readings of the original text from the very best Authorities. The sources from which the Annotations are taken comprise, in the

| OLD TESTAMENT. | APOCRYPHA. | NEW TESTAMENT. |
|---|---|---|
| 90 Commentators, | 49 Commentators, | 78 Commentators, |
| 14 Versions, including the Revised Version, | 20 Versions, | 6 Ancient Versions, 23 Ancient Manuscripts, 11 Critical Editions of the Text, |
| AND | AND | AND |
| R.V. Marginal Readings. | 15 Manuscripts. | Revised Version & Margin. |

The VARIORUM Notes, together with the "*New Aids to Bible Students*" (*see pages* 15-17), give to the ordinary reader of Scripture an amount of information hitherto confined to great scholars and owners of a very costly Library, and comprise the quintessence of Biblical Scholarship in the most convenient form.

The Commentary here is strictly textual (with Brief Explanatory Notes); and the names of the Editors—Professors CHEYNE, DRIVER, SANDAY, the late Rev. P. L. CLARKE, and the Rev. C. J. BALL—are sufficient guarantees for its accuracy and completeness.

*The numerous Commendations of the completed Work include:*—

**The Rev. Dr. Wace,** *Principal of King's College, London :*—
" It is a work of incalculable usefulness, for which the warmest gratitude is due alike to the editors and yourselves."

**The Rev. Canon W. J. Knox Little :**—
" It is a beautiful and valuable work. I think it the most satisfactory copy I have ever had. I like it more, the more I make use of it."

### RETAIL OF ALL BOOKSELLERS.

### GREAT NEW STREET, LONDON, E.C.

# THE VARIORUM APOCRYPHA:

EDITED WITH VARIOUS RENDERINGS AND READINGS FROM THE BEST AUTHORITIES,

BY THE

### REV. C. J. BALL, M.A.,
*Chaplain of Lincoln's Inn.*

Large Type. (Bourgeois 8vo.) Superfine Paper. 276 Pages.

Cloth, bevelled boards, red edges .. .. .. .. .. .. .. .. 6/6
Leather, gilt edges .. .. .. .. .. .. .. .. .. .. 7/6
Leather, round corners, red under gold edges, gold roll inside cover .. .. 8/6
Morocco, boards or limp, gilt edges, gold roll inside cover .. .. .. 13/6
Morocco, limp, round corners, red under gold edges, gold roll inside cover .. 16/-
Levant Yapp, round corners, gilt edges, lined Calf panels .. .. .. .. 24/-

## SOME OPINIONS.

**Guardian:—**
Mr. Ball has worked through a large number of authorities—forty-nine; he has not however confined himself to quoting their opinions, but has added throughout many suggestions of his own, both critical and explanatory.

"The information which he has given is judiciously selected, and the advance marked by his work, on previous works upon the Apocrypha, is exceedingly great."

**Record:—**
"The study of the Apocrypha is gaining ground, and it is a great convenience to have the interpretations of the commentators in so handy a form. Lovers of ancient Jewish literature must heartily thank the editor for placing in their hands so convenient and trustworthy a summary of recent criticism."

**Globe:—**
"The editor has done his work carefully and with knowledge. He contributes an informing preface, and his annotations are to the point."

**Church Review:—**
"This volume, which completes the 'Variorum Bible' is a fitting crown to a task which has done more to explain the *littera scripta* of the Holy Scriptures than any other publication of its kind.

"Mr. Ball's scholarship and researches have brought much light to bear on many obscure passages.

"The number of commentators, versions, and MSS. consulted by the editor is a guarantee of the thoroughness with which he has discharged his task; his name guarantees the ability with which he has done it."

*EYRE & SPOTTISWOODE,*

## VARIORUM APOCRYPHA—continued.

**Expository Times:—**
"Possessors of the 'Variorum Bible' will understand what the Variorum Apocrypha means. There was great need for such an edition of the Apocrypha. The work has been done with patience and good judgment."

**Public Opinion:—**
"Furnishes the general reader with the quintessence of modern and ancient learning bearing on the text."

**Literary World:—**
"Mr. Ball gives us a 'Variorum' edition, embodying not only different readings, but in some cases his own happy emendation of corrupt passages. He gives the poetical parts in metrical form. His edition will be prized by the student, and will stimulate the appetite of the English reader."

**Ecclesiastical Chronicle:—**
"To have all the best renderings focussed, as it were, for ready use, is a privilege every student of the book should appreciate."

**Rock:—**
"It is most convenient for the requirements of the student. It should find a place in every clergyman's library."

**Church Quarterly Review:—**
"One of the greatest difficulties in dealing with the Apocrypha consists in the endeavours to restore the lost original text of books which, for the most part, once existed in the Hebrew tongue. In his preface Mr. Ball points out numerous instances where confusions of similar Hebrew letters have made sheer nonsense of the Greek text.
"The book is a welcome addition to the well-known Variorum Reference Bible."

**Saturday Review:—**
"The books of the Apocrypha, containing as they do much splendid literature, should have the long standing neglect they have suffered removed, by such an edition."

**Queen:—**
"A valuable work."

**Church Times:—**
"Most complete, containing everything having an important bearing on the text."

**Professor E. NESTLE,** the distinguished Septuagint Scholar, writes:—
"Eine Erganzung zur *Variorum Bible*, die nicht genug empfohlen werden kann." —*Theologische Literaturzeitung*, Leipzig, 20 Januar, 1894.
"How splendidly has Ball restored the corrupt text of Judith xvi. 2 (3) by inserting a single letter, ὁ τιθεὶς. Many more examples might be quoted from Ball's *Variorum Apocrypha*."—From Professor E. Nestle's Paper on *The Cambridge Septuagint* (Transactions of The Ninth International Congress of Orientalists).

*GREAT NEW STREET, LONDON, E.C.*

## THE BIBLE READER'S VADE MECUM.

# THE VARIORUM TEACHER'S BIBLE.
With APOCRYPHA. (276 pages.) See p. 10.
## NEW LARGE TYPE EDITION.

*Bourgeois 8vo. (Size, 9⅜ × 6⅞ × 2¼ inches).* 1980 *pages.*

THIS novel and comprehensive Edition of the Authorised Version—the climax towards which the Queen's Printers have consistently developed their Series of Teacher's Bibles during nearly 20 years (1875-1894)—combines—

I.—The VARIORUM Reference Bible. (*See pp.* 9, 10.)

II.—The "AIDS to the Student of the Holy Bible." (*See pp.* 15, 16.)

To the completed *Variorum* Edition of the Reference Bible, the appended "*Aids to the Bible Student*" adds a compendium of Biblical information admitted to be not only the largest and fullest work of the kind, but also the best. The most competent judges have drawn attention to the compass and thoroughness of the "Aids"—none of which are anonymous,—and to the eminence and authority of the contributors.

| *Special Subjects.* | *Authors.* | | *Special Subjects.* |
|---|---|---|---|
| *HISTORY OF BIBLE.* | BALL. | SWETE. LUMBY.* | *PLANTS.* |
| *MUSIC.* | BOSCAWEN. CHEYNE.* | MADDEN. MASKELYNE. | *METALS, &c.* |
| *POETRY.* | DRIVER.* | MAYHEW. | *ANIMAL CREATION.* |
| *MONEY.* | GIRDLESTONE. GREEN. | SANDAY. SAYCE.* | *PROPER NAMES.* |
| *ETHNOLOGY.* | HOLE. HOOKER. | STAINER. TRISTRAM. | *CHRONOLOGY.* |
| *BIBLE & MONUMENTS.* | LEATHES.* | WRIGHT. | *HISTORICAL EPITOME.* |

* Members of Old Testament Revision Committee.

PRICES, Finest India Paper, from 27s. to 52s. 9d.; with APOCRYPHA, 6s. 9d. additional. Thin White Paper, in various leather bindings, from 24s. to 47s. 3d.
**SCHOLASTIC EDITION**, bound in cloth, 18s. 9d.; with APOCRYPHA, 4s. 6d. additional.

## SCHOOL EDITION.
Without APOCRYPHA.

*Nonpareil 8vo. (Size,* 7¾ × 5½ × 1½ *inches.)* 1250 *pages.*

PRICES (Finest India Paper *or* Thin White Paper), from 7s. 6d. to 38s. 6d.

*EYRE & SPOTTISWOODE,*

# THE ADVANTAGES OF THE VARIORUM
### Above every other Bible.
#### For the Variorum TEACHER'S Bible, see page 12.

1. It contains a collection of foot-notes, vastly superior to any that can be found in any one-volume portable Bible.

2. **THE GENERAL READER** unacquainted with the original languages, Hebrew and Greek, is enabled to arrive at a *truer, fuller*, and *deeper* meaning of Scripture than he could obtain from any other published work. The VARIORUM foot-notes correct, explain, unfold, and paraphrase the text; indeed, the alternative versions of obscure or difficult words and phrases often render further note or comment needless.

3. **THE SUNDAY SCHOOL TEACHER** will find the use of the VARIORUM foot-notes of the utmost value to him in the preparation of his lessons. And, whilst teaching, a glance at the foot of the page will enable him to give the *best* alternative reading or translation of the original text, or to explain phrases or special words in the A.V.

    REV. DR. PARKER *says that it is quite as valuable for preachers and hearers as for teachers and scholars. It is a library in itself, containing everything that is immediately needed for the elucidation of the sacred text.*

4. **THE MODERN PREACHER** finds every passage ear-marked of which the text or the translation is considered by scholars defective, and in the corresponding foot-notes he finds the evidence, for and against alterations, judicially digested from the most authoritative Versions and Editions, including the readings and renderings adopted in the Revised Version and its margin. This discrimination of sources and of authorities saves him infinite time and labour. Where all scholars agree upon a rendering the names of authorities are omitted.

    THE ARCHBISHOP OF CANTERBURY says: "*It is so useful that no apology is, I am sure, needed for commending it.*"

5. **THE PROFESSIONAL STUDENT** of the original texts will find in this conspectus a more careful selection of critical data, especially as regards the Old Testament and authorities, than is elsewhere accessible. He will have at hand the very essence of textual criticism, extracted from the most reliable sources, ancient and modern.

    DR. WESTCOTT (LORD BISHOP OF DURHAM) says: "*I constantly use the Old Testament, and find it a great help to have at hand a brief and trustworthy summary of facts and results. Nothing could be better done than the Psalms.*" He also informed the Archbishop of Canterbury and the Conference at Lambeth that he considered that this VARIORUM Edition of the Authorised Version "*was much the best edition of the kind.*"

RETAIL OF ALL BOOKSELLERS.

*GREAT NEW STREET, LONDON, E.C.*

**NEW EDITION (1894), WITH REVISED**

## AIDS TO BIBLE STUDENTS.

### EYRE & SPOTTISWOODE'S
# TEACHER'S BIBLES
(With APOCRYPHA).

*For details see pages 9 to 17.*

**FIFTEEN EDITIONS.**  Prices from 3s. to £2 2s.

In this series of Editions of the Authorised Version—several of them page for page—are combined—

I.—The Queen's Printers' Reference & Variorum Reference Bibles.
II.—The Queen's Printers' "AIDS to the Student of the Holy Bible."

The "*Aids to the Bible Student*" is a compendium of Biblical information admitted to be not only the largest and fullest work of the kind, but also the best. The most competent judges have drawn attention to the compass and thoroughness of the "Aids"—none of which are anonymous,—and to the eminence and authority of the contributors.

| Special Subjects. | Authors. | | Special Subjects. |
|---|---|---|---|
| HISTORY OF BIBLE. | SWETE. | | PLANTS. |
| | BOSCAWEN. | LUMBY.* | |
| MUSIC. | CHEYNE.* | MADDEN. | METALS, &c. |
| POETRY. | GIRDLESTONE. | MASKELYNE. | ANIMAL CREATION. |
| | GREEN. | SANDAY. | |
| MONEY. | HOLE. | SAYCE.* | PROPER NAMES. |
| ETHNOLOGY. | HOOKER. | STAINER | CHRONOLOGY. |
| | LEATHES.* | WRIGHT. | |
| BIBLE & MONUMENTS. | TRISTRAM. | | HISTORICAL EPITOME. |

\* Members of Old Testament Revision Committee.

The AIDS, now approaching their 20th year of publication, have once again been thoroughly revised to date and enlarged.
The work of the Westminster Revisers has been duly collated, and their identifications of words relating to the "ANIMAL CREATION IN THE BIBLE," and "PLANTS OF THE HOLY LAND," have been criticised by the Rev. Dr. TRISTRAM, F.R.S. "THE SUMMARY AND ANALYSIS OF THE BOOKS OF THE OLD TESTAMENT" has been revised and extended by the Rev. Canon R. B. GIRDLESTONE, and "THE REFERENCES IN THE NEW TESTAMENT TO PASSAGES IN THE OLD" by the Rev. Dr. H. B. SWETE.

*Amongst other Additions are the following Articles:—*

THE BIBLE: ITS HISTORY. By Rev. Dr. H. B. SWETE, *Regius Professor of Divinity, Cambridge.*
HEBREW POETRY. By Rev. Canon R. B. GIRDLESTONE, M.A.
THE TESTIMONY OF THE MONUMENTS TO OLD TESTAMENT HISTORY.
By W. ST. CHAD BOSCAWEN, Esq.

*EYRE & SPOTTISWOODE,*

## EYRE & SPOTTISWOODE'S TEACHER'S BIBLES—*continued.*

## SPECIMENS OF TYPES.

### PEARL 24mo.

Or, righteousness. Deut. 24. 13. Ps. 112. 9. Dan. 4. 27. 2 Cor. 9. 9, 10. Or, with. Rom. 12. 8. Or, cause not a trumpet to be sounded.

TAKE heed that ye do not your alms before men, to be seen of them: otherwise ye have no reward of your Father which is in heaven. 2 Therefore when thou doest thine alms, do not sound a trumpet before thee, as the hypocrites do in the synagogues and in the streets, that they may have glory of men. Verily I say unto you, They have their reward.

(SIZE, 5½ × 4¼ × 1⅛ *inches.*)

### MINION 8vo.

2 Or, righteousness. Deut. 24. 13. Ps. 112. 9. Dan. 4. 27. 2 Cor. 9. 9, 10. 3 Or, with. a Rom. 12. 8.

TAKE heed that ye do not your 2 alms before men, to be seen of them: otherwise ye have no reward 3 of your Father which is in heaven.
2 Therefore a when thou doest *thine* alms, 4 do not sound a trumpet before thee, as the hypocrites do in the synagogues and in the streets, that they

(SIZE, 7¼ × 5½ × 1¼ *inches.*)

### RUBY 8vo.

Or, righteousness. Deut. 24. 13. Ps. 112. 9. Dan. 4. 27. 2 Cor. 9. 9, 10. Or, with. a Rom. 12. 8.

TAKE heed that ye do not your alms before men, to be seen of them: otherwise ye have no reward of your Father which is in heaven.
2 Therefore a when thou doest *thine* alms, do not sound a trumpet before thee, as the hypocrites do in the synagogues and in the streets, that they may have glory of men. Verily I say unto you, They have their reward.

(SIZE, 6⅝ × 5½ × 1⅛ *inches.*)

### BREVIER 8vo.

ANNO DOMINI 31.

d Eccles. 5. 2. e 1 Kings 18. 26, 29.

Father which seeth in secret shall reward thee openly.
7 But when ye pray, d use not vain repetitions, as the heathen *do:* e for they think that they shall be heard for their much speaking.
8 Be not ye therefore like unto them: for your Father knoweth

(SIZE, 8¾ × 6 × 2 *inches.*)

## ABRIDGED PRICE LIST.

| DESCRIPTION. | | Cloth. | Leather. | Turkey Morocco. | Turkey Morocco, Circuit. | Levant Morocco, lined Calf, with flaps. | Best Levant, lined Calf, with flaps and Pocket for MSS. |
|---|---|---|---|---|---|---|---|
| Pearl 24mo. | ... | 2/6 | 4/6 | 7/- | 9/- | 11/3 | 17/3 |
| Ruby 8vo. ... | ... | — | 6/- | 9/- | 12/- | 15/- | 22/6 |
| Minion 8vo. | ... | — | 9/6 | 14/- | 18/9 | 19/9 | 30/- |
| Brevier 8vo. | ... | — | 16/6 | 21/9 | 27/- | 28/3 | 37/- |

# THE LARGE TYPE AIDS.

**VARIORUM EDITION, WITH SPECIAL GLOSSARY** (*see p.* 17).

*Bourgeois* 8vo., 388 *pages.* (*Separately.*)

| | s. | d. |
|---|---|---|
| Cloth, bevelled boards, red edges .. .. .. .. .. .. .. .. | 5 | 0 |
| Paste Grain Roan, gilt edges .. .. .. .. .. .. .. .. .. | 8 | 3 |
| Morocco, gilt edges, gold roll inside cover .. .. .. .. .. .. .. | 12 | 6 |

**RETAIL OF ALL BOOKSELLERS.**

*GREAT NEW STREET, LONDON, E.C.*

Special Publications.

# THE AIDS TO BIBLE STUDENTS

JUST COMPLETED

Forms the Second Part of the *VARIORUM* and other Queen's Printers' Teacher's Bibles.

---

THE Queen's Printers were the FIRST TO ISSUE what was known as *the Sunday School Teacher's Bible* in May, 1875. It was not until 16 MONTHS AFTERWARDS that a Bible issued from the Oxford University Press, bearing on its title page "The S. S. Teacher's Edition," and closely following the model of the Queen's Printers' Teacher's Bible; this brief statement is necessary to remove misunderstandings.

The success which attended the publication of the Queen's Printers' Teacher's Bible has been unprecedented. Over One Million Copies have been sold.

This is no doubt due to the fact that "The Aids to Bible Students" were from the outset prepared with the utmost care, in order that the Student might have at his disposal the BEST and SUREST information from the pen of the most Eminent Authority on each of the various subjects treated.

The cordial approval of the principle and contents of former editions by eminent Biblical Scholars, and by the representatives of all classes of Teachers throughout the World, has led to the enlargement of each successive issue, in order to give to the Student THE BEST, MOST RELIABLE, and MOST RECENT information that could be obtained.

In the present issue, very considerable improvements and additions have been made. The Articles have undergone a careful and thorough revision, and, pursuant to recent discoveries, new matter has been added and the whole volume brought up to date. The Aids will therefore be found more than ever PRACTICALLY USEFUL, EXHAUSTIVE IN TREATMENT, and COMPLETE in their character. Several new Articles have been added.

The Publication of the VARIORUM Bible, and of the Revised Version which followed it, called popular attention to the sources from which we have received the Sacred Text, and the quotations in the VARIORUM Notes of Manuscripts, Versions, Ancient Fathers, etc., have aroused a spirit of enquiry as to their relative importance. To meet this, the Rev. Professor Swete has written for these AIDS a new Article entitled,

The Bible: its History.—In this Article, the Rev. Professor Swete places before the Student a summary of the most important results which have been reached by competent enquirers on such questions as the formation and transmission of the original Text, its Versions, Ancient and Modern, etc., etc.

The Bible and its Contents:—OLD TESTAMENT, a valuable summary and analysis of each Book by the Rev. Professor Stanley Leathes, has been further expanded by Canon Girdlestone.

„ THE APOCRYPHA has been summarised and analysed by the Rev. Dr. Wright.

„ THE NEW TESTAMENT Article by Prof. W. Sanday will be found to contain the best results of modern New Testament Scholarship, and his Analyses of the Gospels and Epistles are simply invaluable.

---

*EYRE & SPOTTISWOODE,*

## AIDS TO BIBLE STUDENTS—*continued.*

*Among other important additions may be mentioned:—*

**References in the New Testament to Passages in the Old,** revised and extended by the Rev. Dr. Swete.

**Hebrew Poetry,** by Canon Girdlestone.

**The Testimony of the Monuments to Old Testament History,** by Mr. W. St. Chad Boscawen, who traces from the earliest times many corroborations of Bible History from the Ancient Monuments.

**Metals and Precious Stones,** by Professor N. Story Maskelyne, F.R.S.

**Plants and Animals:**—*Criticisms of their Identifications in the Revised Version,* by the Rev. Canon Tristram, D.D., F.R.S.

**Ethnology of the Bible.**—This Article, treated in four parts, corresponding to four periods in Bible history, viz., the Patriarchal, the Davidic, of the Captivity, and of Christ and His Apostles, as well as the succeeding Article on

**The Bible and the Monuments,** or the Hebrews in their relations with the Oriental Monarchies, have been revised by the Rev. Professor Sayce.

**The Epitome of Bible History** has been minutely revised and extended by the Editor. It is now grouped under four divisions:—1. The Period of the Promises; 2. The Period of Expectation, or Between the Testaments; 3. The Promises fulfilled; 4. The Establishment of the Kingdom of Christ, or the Apostolic History. The Tables alongside the Epitome give the dates of the events, and the references in Scripture.

**The Glossary of Bible Words,** in the Variorum Edition, has been revised and enlarged, and will be found very complete. It refers to the Authorised and Revised Versions, with their marginal readings, and to the Variorum Notes; also to the Apocrypha. It also includes particular names of Plants, Animals, Metals, &c., which formerly appeared under their individual articles, but are now inserted in the Glossary for ready reference.

**The Supplementary Contents, or Key to Subjects,** which indexes the names and words not treated alphabetically elsewhere, will be found of very great use to Teachers.

**The Concordance** (40,000 references) is added, also an Atlas of new Maps, with Index, revised and brought to most recent surveys.

*A List of some of the Contributors to the* **AIDS:**

REV. PROFESSOR SWETE, D.D., *Regius Professor of Divinity, Cambridge.*
REV. PROFESSOR STANLEY LEATHES, D.D., *Professor of Hebrew, King's College, London, &c.*
REV. C. H. H. WRIGHT, D.D., *Examiner in Hebrew, Universities of Oxford, Durham, and London.*
REV. PROFESSOR W. SANDAY, D.D., LL.D., *Dean Ireland's Professor of Exegesis, Oxford.*
REV. PROFESSOR CHEYNE, D.D., *Oriel Professor of Interpretation, Oxford; Canon of Rochester.*
REV. CANON GIRDLESTONE. M.A., *Hon. Canon of Christ Church, Oxford.*
REV. PROFESSOR SAYCE, M.A., LL.D., *Professor of Assyriology, Oxford.*
REV. CANON TRISTRAM, D.D., LL.D., F.R.S., *Durham.*
REV. S. G. GREEN, D.D., *Co-Editor of the Revised English Bible.*
REV. C. H. HOLE, M.A., *Co-Editor of " Smith's Dictionary of Christian Biography," &c.*
PROFESSOR N. STORY MASKELYNE, M.A., F.R.S., *Professor of Mineralogy in the University of Oxford; Hon. Fellow of Wadham College, Oxford.*
W. ST. CHAD BOSCAWEN, F.R.H.S.
SIR J. STAINER, M.A., Mus. Doc., *Professor of Music in the University of Oxford.*
F. W. MADDEN, M.R.A.S., *Author of " History of Jewish Coinage," &c.*
&c. &c. &c.

**RETAIL OF ALL BOOKSELLERS.**

*GREAT NEW STREET, LONDON, E.C.*

## The Queen's Printers'
# VARIORUM and other TEACHER'S BIBLES.

### OPINIONS OF THE CLERGY.

THE ARCHBISHOP OF CANTERBURY (DR. BENSON):—
The Archbishop said, at a Diocesan Conference:—"I should like to call the attention of the Convocation to the New Edition of the 'Variorum Reference Bible,' published by Messrs. Eyre and Spottiswoode. I will just read an account of what it contains. The whole book has been revised. It was laid, I may say, before the Lambeth Conference—the promise of it—and now it is finished. The old edition forms the basis of the new edition; it is printed in larger type; and every passage which has been disputed by great scholars as to its correct translation or rendering, is marked by a figure before and after the sentence or word, these figures referring to the foot-notes, which give the alternative renderings or readings, together with the authorities for the same, abbreviated to save space. The collection of these notes from 69 commentators for the Old Testament, and 73 for the New, has occupied many years close study and preparation. The New Edition is much amplified as compared with the old one, and you may like to know that the opinion of Dr. Westcott is that it is much the best edition of the kind that has appeared."

THE LATE ARCHBISHOP OF YORK (DR. THOMSON):—
"The names of the authors guarantee its excellence. A miniature library of illustrative matter. If such a book is carefully and generally used, there must be a great improvement in Bible knowledge in this generation. The critical matter at the foot of the columns is remarkably complete. *The last feature gives it special value.*"

THE LATE ARCHBISHOP OF ARMAGH:—
"I have carefully examined the 'Variorum Teacher's Bible' published by Messrs. Eyre and Spottiswoode. The varied and valuable amount of information it contains is most remarkable. There are few subjects connected with the Bible left unelucidated. The Student of the Bible will find the Variorum Edition a treasury replete with instruction."

THE BISHOP OF DURHAM (DR. WESTCOTT):—
"Admirably done. I constantly use it."

THE BISHOP OF LIMERICK:—
"The Variorum (Teacher's) Bible, with its References, Concordance, Various Readings and Renderings, and supplemented by its Aids to Students, serves as a Biblical Encyclopædia, useful by its compactness and the value of its contents, to Biblical Students of all grades."

THE BISHOP OF EXETER (DR. BICKERSTETH):—
"I am much gratified with it . . . eminently fitted for teachers, and all who desire in a clear and compendious form very full information respecting the sacred Scriptures.
"A most valuable work, and will greatly enrich the library of Biblical Students."

THE BISHOP OF LLANDAFF:—
"An immense amount of information, a great help to Teachers, and to Bible readers generally.
"The names guarantee the value of the information. I trust it will be largely circulated."

THE BISHOP OF ST. DAVID'S (DR. W. BASIL JONES):—
"I have delayed . . . until I could find more time to look into the volume; it contains so large an amount and variety of matter in a very small space. But its contents appear to me of the highest value and admirable in arrangement. I would refer especially to the various Readings and Renderings in the foot-notes."

*EYRE & SPOTTISWOODE,*

## Special Publications. 19

THE BISHOP OF GLOUCESTER AND BRISTOL:—
"A very valuable work, well suited for those for whom it is designed, and for all earnest students."

THE BISHOP OF LIVERPOOL:—
"I admire it very much, and think it a most valuable edition of the Holy Scriptures. I shall be glad to recommend your work."

THE BISHOP OF WAKEFIELD (DR. WALSHAM HOW):—
"I have carefully examined the (Variorum) Teacher's Bible published by Messrs. Eyre and Spottiswoode, and I consider it a most valuable work. Believing that the Bible is its own best interpreter, I am sure that the aids to an intelligent understanding of the text itself, together with the assistance given to students who desire to have an accurate conception of the purest form of that text, will prove of inestimable service to all Bible readers."

THE BISHOP OF DOWN AND CONNOR:—
"I consider the Variorum Teacher's Bible highly useful both to Teachers and Students. The various readings in the foot-notes largely increase its usefulness, placing before the professional Student an amount of information and research, which to many would otherwise be inaccessible."

THE BISHOP OF CORK:—
"The eminent names of those who have contributed Articles to the Teacher's Aids are a guarantee for the accuracy of the information, which will be found most valuable to those who wish to understand or teach, or first to understand and then to teach, and help to provide that skilled and accurate teaching, which is not only the true antidote to prevalent unbelief, but the great preventive of it."

THE BISHOP OF KILLALOE (DR. FITZGERALD):—
"I find it to be a most perfect compendium of information on almost every Biblical matter that could be comprised within such a compass, and it seems marvellous how much has been introduced and how varied the topics. It will, I am sure, prove a most important aid to Clergymen, Sunday School Teachers, and many others, and I hope to avail myself of it yet in that direction."

THE BISHOP OF TUAM:—
"I admire greatly the most valuable contents."

THE BISHOP OF KILMORE (DR. DARLEY):—
"I have looked through it carefully . . . a most valuable edition of the sacred Scriptures. The Variorum foot-notes represent much critical research, very carefully arranged; the Aids to Bible Students contain a mass of interesting information in a convenient form; useful alike to Teachers and Students."

THE BISHOP OF OSSORY:—
"I feel pleasure in bearing my testimony.
"An invaluable aid both to Clergymen and Teachers, and a marvel of cheapness. The more I have examined it, the more thoroughly have I been satisfied and pleased."

THE RIGHT REV. BISHOP BARRY:—
"For the study of the Text is invaluable."

THE DEAN OF SALISBURY:—
"I am fully sensible of the great boon you have put within the reach of Bible students and it will be my endeavour to promote the knowledge of this valuable edition."

THE DEAN OF ELY:—
"I hope to make use of it, with its various adjuncts of Notes, Readings," &c., &c.

THE DEAN OF LINCOLN:—
"The work will be extremely useful."

THE DEAN OF ROCHESTER (*late Master of Balliol College, Oxford*):—
"A great achievement of toil and thought."

*GREAT NEW STREET, LONDON, E.C.*

THE (LATE) DEAN OF ST. PAUL'S (DR. CHURCH):—
"A wonderful digest of learning. The names of the various scholars are, of course, warrant of care and accuracy, and certainly nothing so complete and comprehensive, in such a compass, has ever before been attempted."

THE DEAN OF PETERBOROUGH:—
"Your Bible strikes me as admirable in every respect. The Various Renderings considerably enhance the value of the work. It will give me very great pleasure to do all in my power to promote the circulation. I know of no one volume to be compared to it for the amount of information it conveys."

THE DEAN OF NORWICH (DR. W. LEFROY, D.D.):—
"There is no work of the kind comparable to this work. It is invaluable."

THE VERY REV. DR. VAUGHAN, *Dean of Llandaff, and (late) Master of the Temple:*—
"I use the Variorum Teacher's Bible with pleasure and profit."

THE DEAN OF LICHFIELD:—
"I am both surprised and delighted at the fulness and accuracy of information to be found in it.
"I will gladly mention it with the approbation which it so well deserves."

THE VERY REV. DR. BUTLER, *Master of Trinity College, Cambridge:*—
"A great achievement."

THE VEN. ARCHDEACON FARRAR:—
"It lies always on my desk. I place a high value upon it."

THE LATE VEN. ARCHDEACON HESSEY:—
"Students of the sacred volume will owe a deep debt to the projectors and producers."

THE REV. CANON BODY:—
"Very well done."

THE REV. CANON KNOX LITTLE:—
"Most useful and helpful."

THE REV. DR. WACE, *of King's College:*—
"A work of incalculable usefulness."

THE LATE REV. DR. EDERSHEIM:—
"It is certainly the best, most complete and useful which has hitherto appeared."

THE REV. DR. SAMUEL G. GREEN:—
"As a companion to the Revised Version it is invaluable."

DR. SALMOND, *of Free College Aberdeen:*—
"I trust it may secure a very wide circulation. The former edition has come to be a familiar book among our students."

THE REV. HUGH PRICE HUGHES:—
"Incomparable and invaluable."

DR. GREENWOOD, *Victoria University (Owen's College), Manchester:*—
"Its merits and remarkable features are already known to me."

THE REV. JOSEPH PARKER, D.D.:—
"I have examined your Bible with great care. It is quite as valuable for preachers and hearers as for Teachers and scholars.
"It is almost a library in itself, containing everything that is immediately needed for the elucidation of the sacred text."

THE BISHOP OF ONTARIO:—
"My opinion of it is nothing so good has hitherto appeared. It is admirably adapted for its purpose of assisting Teachers, and cannot fail to be appreciated by all who are really anxious to find the best instruction in the sacred volume."

THE REV. J. H. VINCENT, *of Chautauqua:*—
"The book is indeed a marvel, a library of learning, a book of books, concerning the 'Book of Books,' and deserves a wide circulation in Europe and America."

*EYRE & SPOTTISWOODE,*

**SPECIAL EDITION** (Lessons Marked in Red), Persian Levant, handsomely tooled, bevelled boards, red under gold edges, **£1 16s. net.**

# The Marked Lectern Bible.

The *Royal 4to. Bible and Apocrypha, with Marginal Marks, printed in red, indicating the Sunday, Holy-day, and Daily Lessons.*

*The Lessons proper for Sundays are marked thus, in red.*
⌊ 1st Sunday in Advent. Morn. ⏤⏤⏤⏤⏤⏤⏤⏤⏤⏤⏤⏀

*The Lessons proper for Holy-days are marked thus, in red.*
⌊ St. Michael, 1st Lesson. Morn. ⌁⌁⌁⌁⌁⌁⌁⌁⌁⌁⌁⏀

*The Daily Lessons are marked thus, in red.*
⌊ January 9. Even. ⏤⏤⏤⏤⏤⏤⏤⏤⏤⏤⏤⏤⏤⏤⏀

*A Calendar to correspond, shows (also at a glance) the pages on which the Lessons occur, thus rendering mistake impossible.*

[PRINTED IN RED.] THIS SYSTEM OF MARKING LEAVES THE TEXT UNTOUCHED.

⌈ Sunday after Ascension Day. Even.
⌊ Queen's Accession.—to v. 10.
⌊ March 31. Even.

N OW after the death of Moses the servant of the LORD it came to pass, that the LORD spake unto Joshua the son of Nun, Moses' minister, saying,

2 Moses my servant is dead; now therefore arise, go over this Jordan, thou, and all this people, unto the land which I do give to them, *even* to the children of Israel.

3 Every place that the sole of your foot shall tread upon, that have I given unto you, as I said unto Moses.

4 From the wilderness and this Lebanon even unto the great river, the river Euphrates, all the land of the Hittites, and unto the great sea toward the going

Chosen for Westminster Abbey; Keble College, Oxford; and 1800 Churches and Cathedrals. Bound in Calf, Morocco, or Levant, prices £3 and upwards.

*GREAT NEW STREET, LONDON, E.C.*

# THE FAMILY BIBLE
## WITH COMMENTARY,

In One Volume. (*Size, 13 × 11 × 3 inches.*)

### With MARGINAL REFERENCES, CONCORDANCE, and INTRODUCTION.

*This work is designed to supply the information needful to an intelligent study of the Holy Scriptures.*

## In Nineteen Thousand Concise Notes
### IT GIVES, IN LARGE TYPE,

I.—A selection from the Various Readings and Translations of the Text.
II.—Explanations of the difficult Words, Phrases, and Passages.
III.—Illustrations, archæological, historical, topographical, from Oriental customs, &c.
IV.—Homiletical comments, original, and selected from Matthew Henry's and similar Commentaries;

AND CONTAINS

## TWELVE STEEL ENGRAVINGS
### Of the Principal PLACES OF INTEREST in the HOLY LAND.

**PRICES.**

|  |  | s. | d. |
|---|---|---|---|
| CB 0. | Cloth, gilt edges | 21 | 0 |
| CB 2. | Leather, gilt sides and back | 31 | 6 |
| CB 12. | Turkey Morocco | 47 | 6 |
| CB 14. | Turkey Morocco, bevelled boards, best, flexible back, red under gold edges | 60 | 0 |
| CB 15. | Best Levant, cushioned boards, solid red under gold edges | 70 | 0 |

RETAIL OF ALL BOOKSELLERS.

*EYRE & SPOTTISWOODE,*

## Special Publications.

POPULAR EDITION OF
THE STANDARD BOOK OF COMMON PRAYER, 1662.

# THE ANNEXED BOOK IN TYPE,
### WITH APPENDICES.

An exact copy, in type, of the Manuscript Book of Common Prayer which was *annexed*, as the authoritative record, to the Act of Uniformity of 1662. In 1891, by special permission of the House of Lords (now the custodians of the MS. Book), H.M. Printers produced by photolithography a *facsimile* of this "Annexed Book," but the work was necessarily too costly for the majority of Churchmen.

To the Type-Edition are appended (I.) A List of Erasures and Corrections in the MS. Book. (II.) A Collation of the MS. Book with "the Convocation Copy" from which it purports to be fairly written. (III.) A Collation with the Authorised Version of Quotations therefrom inserted in the Annexed Book.

**Royal 8vo., Cloth, Bevelled Boards, Red Burnished Edges, price 10s. 6d.**

---

# THE HISTORICAL PRAYER BOOK:
## BEING THE BOOK OF COMMON PRAYER WITH THE SOURCE OF EACH COMPONENT PART AND THE DATE AT WHICH IT WAS INCORPORATED IN THE BOOK STATED IN THE MARGIN.

Edited by the Rev. JAMES CORNFORD, M.A.,
*Lecturer at the London College of Divinity.*

**SPECIALLY PREPARED FOR THE USE OF STUDENTS AND ALL MEMBERS OF THE ESTABLISHED CHURCH.**

Cloth, Red Edges, 5/-

### SOME OPINIONS.

**Globe.**—"The system adopted is excellent."
**Guardian.**—"The work has been done most carefully."
**Record.**—"Welcome to the student of the Prayer Book, or to the average Churchman."
**Leeds Mercury.**—"The edition will be of great use."

Commended also by **The Times**, &c., &c.

**RETAIL OF ALL BOOKSELLERS.**

---

*GREAT NEW STREET, LONDON, E.C.*

## Special Publications.

### FIFTEENTH EDITION.

# THE
# Queen's Printers' Teacher's Prayer Book:

*BEING THE BOOK OF COMMON PRAYER, with INTRODUCTIONS, ANALYSES, NOTES, and a COMMENTARY UPON THE PSALTER.*

BY THE

### RIGHT REV. ALFRED BARRY, D.D.,
*Canon of Windsor,*
*Late Bishop of Sydney and Metropolitan Primate of Australia and Tasmania;*

AND A

**GLOSSARY by the Rev. A. L. MAYHEW, M.A.**

The "Teacher's Prayer Book," now so well known, is the only work of the kind published in a popular form at popular prices. It is issued in two sizes, 24mo. and 16mo., and in various bindings (*see School Edition and Prices below*).

In the arrangement of the work the most simple plan has been adopted, the Prayer Book and its explanation being interpaged throughout; and the work of Dr. BARRY as Editor makes it of such standard value as to entitle it to rank as a companion-volume to the Queen's Printers' "Teacher's Bibles."

|  | 24mo. EDITION. | 16mo. EDITION. |
|---|---|---|
|  | s. d. | s. d. |
| Cloth boards, red edges | 3 6 | 6 0 |
| Leather, limp, gilt edges | 4 6 | 7 6 |
| Leather, round corners, red under gold edges, and gold roll inside cover | 5 6 | 8 4 |
| Polished Persian Calf, limp, round corners, red under gold edges, and gold roll inside cover | 5 8 | 9 0 |
| Morocco, limp, gilt edges | 6 6 | 9 0 |
| Morocco, boards, gilt edges | 7 0 | 9 6 |
| Morocco, circuit | 8 0 | 12 0 |
| Morocco, limp, round corners, red under gold edges, and gold roll inside cover | 7 6 | 12 0 |

**SCHOOL EDITION** (without Commentary on Psalter and Glossary), price 2/6.

RETAIL OF ALL BOOKSELLERS.

*EYRE & SPOTTISWOODE,*

Special Publications.

## A SELECT
# GLOSSARY
### of Bible Words
### AND
### Words and Phrases in the Prayer Book.

With References to the Text and Illustrative Passages from English Classical Authors, containing obsolete expressions, especially in Psalms, as well as Theological, Ecclesiastical, and Liturgical Terms, with Explanations and Etymologies,

### BY REV. A. L. MAYHEW, M.A.,
*Chaplain of Wadham College, Oxford.*

**PRICES.**

| | |
|---|---|
| Cloth, gilt edges . . . . . . . . . . . | 2/- |
| Paste Grain Roan, gilt edges . . . . . . . . . . | 3/- |
| Morocco, limp, gilt edges . . . . . . . . . | 7/6 |

*LARGE TYPE. For the Aged and Infirm.*

# THE PSALTER with COMMENTARY,
### From the Teacher's Prayer Book,
**BY**
The Right Rev. ALFRED BARRY, D.D.

*Size, 8½ × 7 × 1 inches.*

The Introduction to the Psalter is included, the main purpose of which —as prefatory to the special annotations on each Psalm—is to examine the general character, style, and structure of the Psalter, especially in relation to its use in the service of the Church in all ages.

**Prices and Bindings.**

| | |
|---|---|
| Cloth boards, red edges, burnished . . . . . . | 3/6 |
| Leather, round corners, red under gold edges . . . . . | 7/6 |
| Turkey Morocco, limp, ditto, ditto, gold roll inside cover . . . | 12/6 |

**RETAIL OF ALL BOOKSELLERS.**

*GREAT NEW STREET, LONDON, E.C.*

Fiftieth Thousand.

**SARAH WILSON'S HYMNS FOR CHILDREN.** Price 1s.
With Music by Sir ARTHUR SULLIVAN. Exquisitely Illustrated by JANE M. DEALY and FRED. MARRIOTT.

*ILLUSTRATIONS.*

1. Children Conversing. By Dealy.
2. Landscape, with Cattle. By Marriott.
3. Child and Seascape. By Dealy.
4. Riverside Scene. By Marriott.
5. Child at Prayer. By Dealy.
6. Indian Girl Reading. By Dealy.
7. Garden Scene. By Marriott.
8. Two Boys. By Dealy.
9. Moonlight Scene. By Marriott.
10. Girl at Devotion. By Dealy.
and
Vignette Views of Jerusalem, &c. &c.

**CHILDREN'S PRAYERS.** One Hundredth Thousand. One Shilling. By same Author. Illustrated by the same Artists.
In Specially Designed Covers, Rounded Corners, Small Quarto.

---

Cloth, Bevelled, 2s. 6d., and in Superior Bindings.

**THE IMITATION OF CHRIST.** By THOMAS À KEMPIS. (Revised Translation.) New Edition. Square 16mo.
With Preface by the Rev. W. J. KNOX LITTLE, M.A., Canon Residentiary of Worcester, and Vicar of Hoar Cross.
Handsomely printed, with Red-lined Borders, on Toned Paper.

**CHRISTIAN YEAR, HOLY LIVING, AND HOLY DYING** can be had uniform in Style and Price with the above.

---

**THE RHYTHM OF S. BERNARD.** Just published, Edition de Luxe, with Twelve full-page Illustrations. (NEALE'S Translation.) Including "JERUSALEM THE GOLDEN," and "FOR THEE, O DEAR, DEAR COUNTRY." Crown 4to. 5s.

Church Times:—"A veritable edition de luxe, beautifully printed."

---

**OLD BIBLES:** An Account of the Various Versions of the English Bible, and of their notable Editions. By J. R. DORE. Describes the slow and gradual steps whereby the Authorised Version was reached. Half Bound, Vellum Cloth, Red Burnished Edges, 5s.

The Bishop of Lincoln:—"An interesting and valuable volume."

---

(SECOND EDITION.)

**THE BATTLE OF THE STANDPOINTS:** In Controversion of the Higher Criticism. By ALFRED CAVE, B.A., D.D., Principal and Professor of Systematic Theology of Hackney College; Author of "The Inspiration of the Old Testament Inductively Considered"; &c., &c.
Prices: Paper Covers, 6d.; Cloth Boards, Red Edges, 1s.

---

*EYRE & SPOTTISWOODE.*

www.ingramcontent.com/pod-product-compliance
Lightning Source LLC
Chambersburg PA
CBHW031742230426
**43669CB00007B/448**